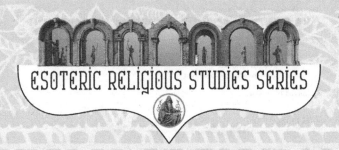

ESOTERIC RELIGIOUS STUDIES SERIES

THEURGY

AND NEOPLATONIC MYSTICISM

BOOK #6

Esoteric Religious Studies Series
THEURGY
AND NEOPLATONIC MYSTICISM

Author: Diohka Aesden
Publisher: Cineris Multifacet
Publication Date: 2023
ISBN: - 979-8-85-338673-0 (Paperback)
-

For inquiries and permissions, please contact:
    Cineris Multifacet
    cinerismultifacet@gmail.com

Design and Typesetting:
    Cineris Multifacet

Cover Design:
    Cineris Multifacet

Disclaimer:

Manufactured in the United States of America

First Edition: 2023

ISBN-13: 979-8-85-338673-0 (Paperback)
-

19   54   95

This page left intentionally blank.

OTHER BOOKS IN THIS SERIES

A WORLD OF ESOTERIC THOUGHT

ESOTERIC RELIGIOUS STUDIES SERIES

THEURGY
AND NEOPLATONIC
MYSTICISM

Dedicated to

The Seven Planetary Spheres

and to

Pope Philo III

A

ALPHA

May the reader of the **Esoteric Religious Studies Series** be blessed abundantly. We extend our heartfelt gratitude for your engagement with this sagacious study of esoteric traditions. As you adventure through the pages, may your mind be illuminated with knowledge and your heart be filled with *wisdom*. May the insights and revelations within these texts expand your understanding and bring clarity to your spiritual path. May you be well-informed, enriched, and guided by the sacred *wisdom* that unfolds before you. May this series be a source of inspiration, transformation, and blessings upon your life.

If you enjoy the words of this book, please consider leaving a review in the marketplace you found it so that its content can reach even more interested individuals.

Please visit the author page of Diohka Aesden to keep up with new releases on religion, esoterica, mythology, and other related topics.

TABLE OF CONTENTS

A

$$\Omega$$

INTRODUCTION

Theurgy and Neoplatonic mysticism are two interlaced and revelatory philosophical and spiritual traditions that have left a lasting effect on the course of Western thought and mysticism. Ineradicable from the teachings of the ancient Greek philosopher Plato and further developed by later Neoplatonists like Plotinus, these traditions dive into the nature of the divine, the soul, and the ways to achieve union with the higher realms.

This exploration will traverse into a valuable atlas of topics related to *theurgy* and Neoplatonic mysticism. From the concept of *divine hierarchy* and the place of *theurgy* in Neoplatonic philosophy to the use of *symbols*, rituals, and divine names, we will start on a quest through the depths of these mystical practices and their influence on the human experience.

The first step on our quest involves understanding the concept of *divine hierarchy*. Within Neoplatonic thought, there exists a hierarchical order of realities, emanating from *the One*, the ineffable source of all existence. As the divine emanates, it gives rise to different levels of existence, each representing a greater degree of perfection and beauty. *Theurgy* acts as a means to traverse this *divine hierarchy*, enabling individuals to ascend and attain closer communion with the ultimate source.

At the heart of *theurgy* lies the notion of achieving union with the divine. The ancient Greek term "*theourgia*" signifies the divine *work* or divine *action*, and the theurgist seeks to invoke and commune with *divine beings*, *angels*, and *deities* to experience this union. Through spiritual practices, rituals, and invocations, the practitioner wants to go beyond the bounds of the material world and reach higher states of consciousness, where *divine union* becomes a tangible reality.

To understand the place of *theurgy* in Neoplatonic philosophy, we dive into the teachings of Plotinus, the influential Neoplatonist philosopher of the 3rd century CE. Plotinus posits that the ultimate goal of human life is to attain a union with *the One*, the divine principle beyond all existence. *Theurgy* holds a significant place in this process, acting as a means to purify the soul, elevate consciousness, and facilitate the direct experience of divine reality.

Symbols and rituals hold great importance in *theurgy*, acting as bridges between the mundane and the *divine realms*. The use of sacred *symbols* and ritualistic practices helps align the practitioner with higher spiritual forces, enabling them to experience the *divine energies*. *Theurgy* acknowledges the power of intention and symbolic acts, where spiritual importance is infused into mundane actions, inviting *divine presence* into daily life.

The quest of the soul through different realms forms a central theme in *theurgy* and Neoplatonic mysticism. *Metempsychosis*, the concept of the soul's transmigration or reincarnation, underpins the idea of the *soul's quest* through various lifetimes. *Theurgy* provides practices that help the soul prepare for this quest, purify its essence, and ultimately liberate it from the cycle of birth and death.

Theurgy's influence on *art, architecture, music,* and literature cannot be overlooked. Breathed by the principles of *divine beauty* and *transcendence,* artists and creators have tried to channel *divine energies* into their works, infusing them with spiritual importance. These forms of expression serve as portals to higher realities, inviting the audience to experience a glimpse of the *divine presence.*

The relationship between *theurgy* and *astrology* also emerges as an intriguing aspect of these mystical traditions. *Astrology,* the study of celestial bodies' movements and their influence on human affairs, aligns with the notion of cosmic harmony and *divine order. Theurgy* complements *astrology* by invoking celestial powers and aligning with the cosmic rhythms to attain higher states of consciousness.

Talismans and *amulets,* imbued with spiritual energies, find a place in *theurgical practices.* These objects serve as protective charms, harnessing the power of *divine forces* to shield the wearer from malevolent influences and attract blessings and guidance. The use of *talismans* and *amulets* demonstrates *theurgy*'s belief in the relationship of spiritual energies within the material world.

Theurgy's connection to *divination* and *prophecy* unveils another facet of its potential. The practitioner seeks to attune to higher dimensions of consciousness, gaining insights into future events and hidden truths. Theurgical techniques for *divination* enable the individual to glimpse into the nexus of destiny and make informed choices aligned with higher guidance.

The *soul's quest* through different realms is complemented by the concepts of *divine transcendence and immanence* within *theurgy*. *Theurgy* acknowledges the simultaneous existence of the divine beyond the material world (*transcendence*) and its immanent presence within all things. By recognizing the enmeshment of all life, *theurgy* nurtures a sense of reverence and responsibility toward the divine creation.

Theurgy's place in Neoplatonic theories of evil and the demonic dives into the presence of negative influences within the cosmic order. *Theurgy's* practices for spiritual protection and defense come into play to safeguard the practitioner from malevolent forces and restore harmony within the *soul's quest*.

Ethics and moral philosophy find a deep resonance in *theurgical practices*. *Theurgy* highlights the cultivation of virtues and ethical alignment as essential for attuning with *divine energies*. By embodying *divine qualities*, the practitioner contributes to the establishment of a harmonious and just world.

The concept of divine revelation lies at the core of *theurgy*. *Theurgical practices* aim to unveil hidden truths and mystical insights beyond the ordinary perception. Through communion with the divine, the practitioner gains access to revelatory wisdom and revelations that guide their spiritual quest.

Theurgy's techniques for achieving altered states of consciousness provide avenues for revelatory spiritual experiences. By transcending ordinary awareness, the practitioner connects with higher dimensions of reality, encountering the divine directly. These altered states serve as gateways to expanded understanding and higher truths.

In Neoplatonic theories of knowledge and epistemology, *theurgy* highlights direct experiential knowledge as superior to mere intellectual understanding. Through *theurgy*, the individual gains direct insights into the divine and the higher realities, surpassing intellectual comprehension.

Theurgy-breathed theories of beauty and aesthetics celebrate *divine beauty* as the ultimate source of all aesthetic experiences. Artists and creators draw from the *divine source*, infusing their works with spiritual depth and beauty.

Divine love holds a central place in *theurgy*, as it is the driving force behind the soul's longing for union with the divine. *Theurgy* kindles the fire of *divine love* within the practitioner, triggering them to seek communion with the higher realms.

Divine grace emerges as a necessary concept in *theurgy*, signifying the benevolent and unmerited favor of the divine. *Theurgy* provides practices to invoke and receive divine grace, encouraging a revelatory sense of *divine presence* and guidance.

Theurgical techniques for spiritual *purification* and transformation offer paths to go beyond the bounds of the ego and align with divine virtues. Through *purification*, the soul becomes a vessel for *divine energies*, leading to revelatory spiritual transformation.

The concept of *divine light* acts as a *symbol* of higher consciousness and spiritual illumination. *Theurgy* invokes and channels *divine light*, leading to revelatory experiences of enlightenment and the revelation of higher truths.

Divine order stands for the harmonious arrangement of the cosmos and the relationship of spiritual forces. *Theurgy* aligns with this *divine order*, attuning the practitioner to higher rhythms and facilitating spiritual growth.

Neoplatonic theories of the afterlife explore the *soul's quest* beyond physical death. *Theurgy* prepares the soul for this quest, facilitating ascent to higher realms, and ensuring a favorable afterlife.

In culmination, *theurgy* and Neoplatonic mysticism combine an atlas of revelatory philosophical and spiritual insights, inviting individuals to explore the depths of *divine connection*. By engaging in *theurgical practices*, individuals seek to go beyond the bounds of the material world, purify their souls, and achieve union with the divine. The concepts explored here illuminate the transformative power of *theurgy* and its lasting influence on the human quest for higher truths and spiritual realization.

I: DIVINE HIERARCHY

The concept of the "*Divine Hierarchy*" is a central aspect of Neoplatonic thought. It refers to the hierarchical structure of *divine beings* and the emanation of reality from the ultimate principle, *the One*, down to the material world. This concept was developed and elaborated upon by various Neoplatonic philosophers, including Plotinus, Proclus, and Iamblichus.

In Greek, the term for the *Divine Hierarchy* is "Θεία Ιεραρχία" (*Theia Hierarchia*). *Theia* means "*divine*," and *Hierarchia* refers to a hierarchy or sacred order. The *Divine Hierarchy* describes the arrangement and relationship of different levels of *divine beings*, each representing a distinct aspect of reality and participating in the *divine emanation*.

At the highest level of the *Divine Hierarchy* stands *the One*, also known as "Το Εν" (*To Hen*) in Greek, which means "*The One*" in English. *The One* is the ultimate transcendent principle, the source of all existence and the highest form of unity. It is beyond description and comprehension and is the ultimate goal of mystical union and ascent.

From *the One*, there emanates a series of *divine beings*, each representing a lower level in the hierarchy. These beings are known as "Νοεροί" (*Noeroi*) or "*Intellects*" in Greek. They are often described as *divine minds* or *intelligences* that possess knowledge and understanding of the *divine realms*. The *Noeroi* are in a state of perfect *contemplation* and unity with *the One*.

Below the *Noeroi*, there exists another level in the hierarchy, known as "Ψυχή" (*Psyche*) in Greek, which means "*Soul*" in English. The *Soul* stands for the intermediate world between the divine and the material world. It is seen as the mediator between the intelligible and the sensible realms. The *Soul* is associated with movement, life, and the principle of harmony.

Within the *Soul*, there are further divisions or levels referred to as "Λόγοι" (*Logoi*) or "*Forms*" in Greek. These *Logoi* are archetypal principles or ideas that serve as the patterns for the manifestation of individual things in the material world. They are the source of order, beauty, and intelligibility in the cosmos.

The next level in the *Divine Hierarchy* is the world of the celestial gods, known as "Θεοί" (*Theoi*) or "*Gods*" in Greek. These celestial gods are associated with the heavenly bodies, like the sun, moon, and planets. They govern the cosmic processes and play a significant place in the *divine order* and *providence*.

Below the celestial gods, there exists the world of *daimones*, referred to as "Δαίμονες" (*Daimones*) in Greek, which means "*Daimons*" in English. *Daimones* are intermediate beings between gods and humans. They are seen as divine messengers, guardians, and mediators, responsible for the communication between the divine and human realms.

Finally, at the lowest level of the *Divine Hierarchy*, there is the material world or the world of "Ύλη" (*Hyle¹*) in Greek, which means "*Matter*" in English. This is the world of physical bodies, subject to change and imperfection. The material world is determined the furthest removed from the *divine source* and is associated with limitation and multiplicity.

The *Divine Hierarchy* is not viewed as a static structure but as a dynamic process of emanation and return. The emanation begins with *the One*, and each level of the hierarchy proceeds from the level above it. The return, on the other hand, involves the ascent of the soul through the levels of the hierarchy, leading back to the ultimate union with *the One*.

The *Divine Hierarchy* has revelatory implications for spiritual practice and mystical ascent. It provides a scaffold-

---

1 See "Gnosticism: Ancient Mystical Traditions, Sects & Texts" - Chapter VIII: Hylics, Psychics, and Pneumatics in Gnosticism.

ing for understanding reality and the path to spiritual enlightenment. The goal of the practitioner is to go beyond the
bounds of the material world and ascend through the levels
of the *hierarchy*, ultimately attaining union with *the One*.

In culmination, the concept of the *Divine Hierarchy*
in Neoplatonic thought outlines the hierarchical structure of
divine beings and the emanation of reality from *the One* to the
material world. It is a fundamental aspect of Neoplatonic
philosophy and provides a scaffolding for understanding the
nature of the cosmos and the path to spiritual realization. By
exploring the *Divine Hierarchy*, individuals can deepen their
understanding of Neoplatonic mysticism and its revelatory
insights into the nature of the divine and the soul.

II: ACHIEVING UNION WITH THE DIVINE

Theurgy, known as "Θεουργία" (*Theourgia*) in Greek, is a central concept in Neoplatonic philosophy and mysticism. It refers to a spiritual practice or discipline aimed at achieving union with the divine and participating in the activities of the gods. The term itself combines "*theos*" meaning "*god*" and "*ergon*" meaning "*work*" or "*action*." *Theurgy* is often seen as a means of bridging the gap between the human and the divine, allowing individuals to experience a revelatory connection with higher realms of existence.

In Neoplatonic thought, *theurgy* is determined a sacred and transformative activity that enables individuals to participate in the divine life and ultimately attain a state of union with the divine. The goal of *theurgy* is not merely intellectual understanding or *contemplation* but an experiential and participatory engagement with the divine realities.

The practice of *theurgy* involves a variety of techniques, rituals, and spiritual exercises designed to invoke and commune with *divine beings*. These practices include prayer, *meditation, contemplation*, the recitation of sacred names and hymns, the performance of specific gestures and movements, and the use of symbolic objects and *talismans*.

Central to theurgical practice is the *invocation* of *deities* and angelic beings. By calling upon the divine entities, practitioners seek their presence and guidance in their spiritual quest. These invocations are often accompanied by rituals and ceremonies that create a sacred and conducive environment for *divine communion*.

Theurgy also highlights the *purification* of the soul as a prerequisite for union with the divine. *Purification* involves the removal of negative emotions, desires, and attachments that hinder spiritual progress. It is believed that a pure and virtuous soul is more receptive to the *divine presence* and can ascend to higher levels of consciousness.

One of the key figures in the development of *theurgical practices* is Iamblichus, a Neoplatonic philosopher of the late 3rd and early 4th century. Iamblichus emphasized the use of *symbols, talismans*, and rituals in *theurgy*. He viewed theurgic practices as a means of harnessing and channeling divine power and energy for spiritual transformation.

According to Iamblichus, *theurgical practices* involve the participation in the *divine energies* and activities, which leads to a mystical union with the divine. This union is not a merging of identities but a transcendent state of consciousness where the individual becomes one with the divine while still maintaining their individuality.

Theurgy is often seen as a complement to philosophy in Neoplatonic thought. While philosophy seeks intellectual understanding and *contemplation* of the divine, *theurgy* provides a more direct and experiential encounter with the divine. It bridges the gap between the human and the divine by allowing individuals to actively engage with the divine realities.

The Neoplatonic philosopher Plotinus also discussed the concept of *theurgy* in his works. He emphasized the importance of the soul's ascent to the divine and the ultimate union with *the One*. Plotinus believed that *theurgy* was a means of purifying the soul, liberating it from the bounds of the material world, and enabling it to partake in the *divine essence*.

In the Neoplatonic tradition, *theurgy* is often associated with the concept of "divine illumination" or "theoria." Theoria refers to a direct and intuitive vision of the divine realities that goes beyond ordinary human perception. It is determined a transformative and ecstatic experience that brings individuals closer to the divine.

Theurgical practices were not limited to individuals but also extended to communities and cities. Theurgic rituals and ceremonies were performed to ensure the wellness and harmony of the community as a whole. They were believed to attract divine blessings and protect against negative influences.

It is important to note that *theurgy* is distinct from magic in Neoplatonic thought. While magic aims to manipulate and control the natural and supernatural forces for personal gain, *theurgy* seeks a harmonious and participatory communion with the divine. *Theurgy* is grounded in a deep reverence for the divine and a recognition of the inherent order and goodness in the cosmos.

In culmination, *theurgy* is a revelatory and transformative spiritual practice within Neoplatonic philosophy and mysticism. It offers a means of achieving union with the divine and participating in the activities of the gods. Through rituals, invocations, and *purification*, individuals seek to go beyond their human bounds and experience a direct and transformative encounter with the divine realities. *Theurgy* is seen as a path to spiritual enlightenment, union with the divine, and the attainment of a higher state of consciousness.

III: THE NEOPLATONIC PHILOSOPHY OF PLOTINUS

The place of *theurgy* in the Neoplatonic philosophy of Plotinus is significant and multifaceted. Plotinus, one of the most influential Neoplatonic philosophers of the 3rd century, developed a comprehensive
system of thought that aimed to reconcile the teachings
of Plato with mystical and religious elements. While
Plotinus primarily focused on philosophical *contemplation* and intellectual understanding, he also acknowledged the importance of *theurgical practices* as a means
of achieving union with the divine.

In Greek, the term for *theurgy* is
"Θεουργία" (*Theourgia*), derived from "*theos*" meaning
"*god*" and "*ergon*" meaning "*work*" or "*action.*" *Theurgy* in
Plotinus' philosophy refers to the spiritual practice of
invoking and communing with *divine beings* to attain a
higher state of consciousness and participate in the activities of the gods.

Plotinus viewed *theurgy* as a transformative
and contemplative activity that enabled individuals to
go beyond the bounds of the material world and establish a connection with higher realms of existence. For

him, *theurgy* played an important place in bridging the gap between the human and the divine, allowing individuals to experience a revelatory union with the *divine essence.*

While Plotinus emphasized philosophical *contemplation* as the primary means of attaining knowledge and understanding of the divine, he recognized the value of *theurgical practices* in facilitating direct experiences and encounters with the divine realities. He determined *theurgy* as a complementary discipline to philosophy, providing a more experiential and participatory engagement with the divine.

According to Plotinus, the ultimate goal of human life is the mystical union with *the One*, the transcendent principle from which all existence emanates. Plotinus believed that through the practice of *theurgy*, individuals could ascend from the lower realms of material existence to higher levels of consciousness, eventually reaching the *divine source* itself.

Plotinus viewed *theurgy* as a transformative process that involved purifying the soul and elevating it to higher levels of being. He believed that the soul, by its nature, longs for union with the divine and seeks to return to its *divine origin*. *Theurgy* was seen as a means of awakening this innate longing and facilitating the soul's ascent to its true home.

Theurgy, in Plotinus' philosophy, involved the *invocation* of *divine beings* and the participation in their activities. By invoking the gods and engaging in theurgical rituals, individuals tried to establish a connection with the divine and partake in the *divine essence*. These rituals often included the recitation of *sacred hymns*, the use of symbolic gestures and objects, and the cultivation of a contemplative and receptive state of mind.

Plotinus saw *theurgy* as a transformative process that led to the *purification* of the soul and the liberation from the bounds of the material world. Through the practice of *theurgy*, individuals could go beyond the world of multiplicity and ascend to the world of unity and oneness with the divine.

While Plotinus emphasized the importance of philosophical *contemplation*, he recognized that not all individuals were capable of attaining intellectual understanding of the divine through philosophy alone. *Theurgical practices* offered an alternative path for those who were more inclined towards experiential and symbolic approaches to spirituality.

In Plotinus' philosophy, *theurgy* was not determined a means of acquiring supernatural powers or controlling *divine forces* for personal gain. Instead, it was viewed as a sacred and reverential engagement with the divine, driven by a genuine love and longing for union with the *divine essence. Theurgy* was seen as a path of devotion, surrender, and self-*transcendence.*

Plotinus also emphasized the importance of virtue and moral *purification* in *theurgical practices.* He believed that individuals needed to encourage virtues and rid themselves of negative emotions and desires to establish a closer connection with the divine. Moral *purification* was seen as a prerequisite for the successful practice of *theurgy* and the attainment of union with the divine.

While Plotinus did not provide detailed instructions or specific techniques for *theurgical practices*,
he acknowledged their transformative power and their
ability to elevate the soul to higher states of consciousness. He determined *theurgy* as a sacred and awe-triggering process that transcended ordinary human existence and allowed individuals to participate in the divine life.

In culmination, *theurgy* played a significant
place in the Neoplatonic philosophy of Plotinus. While
he primarily emphasized philosophical *contemplation* as
the means of attaining knowledge of the divine, he also
recognized the value of *theurgical practices* in facilitating
direct encounters with the divine. *Theurgy* was viewed
as a transformative and contemplative activity that
enabled individuals to go beyond the bounds of the material world and achieve union with the *divine essence*. It
was seen as a path of devotion, moral *purification*, and
self-*transcendence*, leading individuals closer to the ultimate goal of mystical union with *the One*.

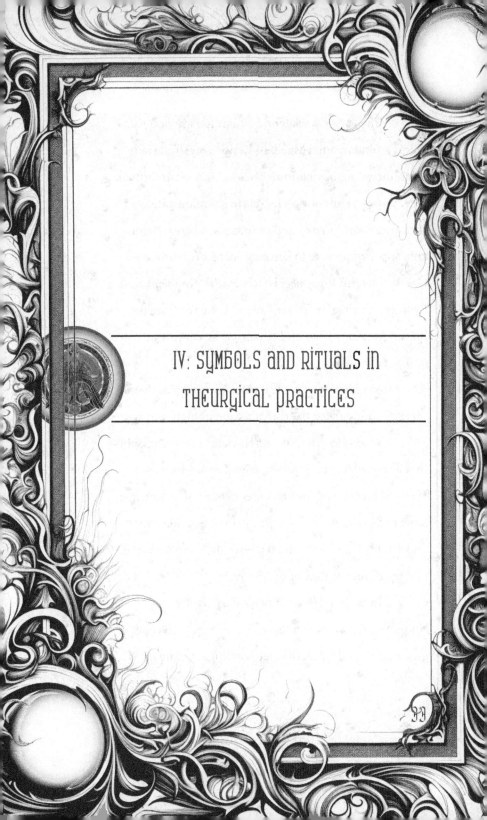

IV: Symbols and Rituals in Theurgical Practices

The use of *symbols* and rituals in *theurgical practices* is a fundamental aspect of various mystical traditions, including Neoplatonic *theurgy*. *Symbols* and rituals serve as powerful tools to facilitate communication with the divine, invoke higher forces, and create a sacred space conducive to spiritual transformation. In Greek, the term for *symbol* is "σύμβολον" (*sýmbolon*), and the term for *ritual* is "τελετή" (*teleti*). Let us explore the importance of *symbols* and rituals in the context of *theurgical practices*.

Symbols play a central place in *theurgy* as they serve as conduits for the transmission of higher truths and *divine energies*. They are often visual representations that encapsulate revelatory spiritual concepts, archetypal forces, and hidden meanings. *Symbols* have the power to evoke deep emotions, stir the imagination, and establish a connection between the conscious mind and the deeper realms of the *psyche*.

In *theurgy*, *symbols* are used to invoke and communicate with *divine beings*, activate specific energies, and align the practitioner with higher realities.

They act as focal points for concentration and *contemplation*, enabling the practitioner to enter into a state of resonance with the *divine forces* they represent.

Various *symbols* are employed in *theurgical practices*, including sacred geometrical forms, celestial bodies, divine names and sigils, elemental representations, and mythological images. For example, the use of the *pentagram* as a *symbol* in *theurgy* stands for the five elements and the human microcosm's alignment with the divine macrocosm.

Rituals are an integral part of *theurgical practices* as they provide a structured scaffolding for engaging with the divine and creating a sacred space. Rituals involve specific actions, gestures, words, and sequences that have symbolic importance and invoke spiritual energies. They often follow a prescribed set of procedures and are performed with intention and reverence.

Rituals in *theurgy* serve several purposes. Firstly, they establish a ritualistic scaffolding that helps individuals focus their attention and enter into a state of heightened awareness. The repetitive and symbolic nature of rituals creates a sense of rhythm, establishing a connection between the individual and the divine.

Secondly, rituals in *theurgy* serve as a means of *purification* and preparation. They involve the use of ritualistic gestures, like purifying with water or incense, which symbolically cleanse the practitioner and create a state of inner and outer purity. This *purification* is necessary to establish a receptive state of mind and facilitate the connection with the divine.

Furthermore, rituals in *theurgy* often include the recitation of prayers, invocations, and *sacred hymns*. These spoken or chanted words carry vibrational energy and sacred intent, allowing the practitioner to establish a direct connection with the *divine beings* being invoked. The power of sound and vibration is believed to align the practitioner's consciousness with higher frequencies and open channels of communication with the divine.

The physical actions performed in rituals also have symbolic importance. For instance, gestures like raising the hands in supplication or extending them in a welcoming manner symbolize the individual's openness and receptivity to *divine energies*. Similarly, movements like circumambulation[2] (walking in a circular path) represent the cyclical nature of cosmic existence and the practitioner's alignment with the *divine order*.

The timing and sequencing of rituals also hold importance in *theurgical practices*. Certain celestial alignments, planetary hours, or specific dates may be determined more auspicious for performing rituals. These temporal aspects are believed to enhance the resonance with the *divine forces* and align the practitioner with specific energetic influences.

Moreover, rituals in *theurgy* often incorporate the use of symbolic objects and tools. These objects, like *ritual* knives, chalices, wands, and *amulets*, hold symbolic meanings and serve as extensions of the practitioner's intention and will. They can be charged with specific energies and act as intermediaries between the mundane and the *divine realms*.

---

[2] See "Sufism: Persian Mystical Path of Islam" - Chapter III: Purification of the Soul: Exploring Islamic Rituals and Spiritual Practices.

Theurgical rituals may take various forms, ranging from private individual practices to communal ceremonies. In communal settings, rituals encourage a sense of unity and collective participation in the divine. They create a shared sacred experience, amplifying the collective intention and invoking the presence of the *divine beings* in a more potent manner.

It is important to note that *symbols* and rituals in *theurgy* are not meant to be performed mechanically or as empty gestures. They are conduits through which the practitioner engages with the deeper layers of reality and establishes a conscious connection with the divine. The sincerity, devotion, and inner alignment of the practitioner are necessary for the efficacy of the *symbols* and rituals.

Symbols and rituals in *theurgy* are not limited to specific cultural or religious traditions. They draw upon universal archetypal patterns and vibe with the deeper structures of the human *psyche*. Thus, the choice of *symbols* and the design of rituals may vary according to personal inclination, cultural background, and the specific aims of the practitioner.

In culmination, the use of *symbols* and rituals in *theurgical practices* holds an important place in establishing a connection with the divine and facilitating spiritual transformation. *Symbols* act as conduits for higher truths and energies, while rituals provide a structured scaffolding for engaging with the divine and creating a sacred space. Together, *symbols* and rituals in *theurgy* help practitioners focus their attention, align with higher realities, and establish a conscious connection with the *divine forces* they seek to invoke.

V: purification and asceticism

The importance of *purification* and *asceticism* in *theurgy* is a significant aspect of spiritual practice within various mystical traditions, including Neoplatonic *theurgy*. *Purification* and *asceticism* are seen as essential preparatory steps that enable individuals to establish a deeper connection with the divine and elevate their consciousness to higher realms. In Greek, the term for *purification* is "κάθαρσις" (*kátharsis*) and the term for *asceticism* is "ασκηση" (*askísi*).

Purification, or *katharsis*, involves the removal of impurities, distractions, and negative influences that hinder spiritual progress. It is a process of cleansing and purging the soul, mind, and body, creating a state of inner clarity, receptivity, and harmony. *Purification* is determined necessary as it allows the practitioner to approach the divine with a purified intention and an open heart.

In the context of *theurgy*, *purification* acts multiple purposes. Firstly, it helps individuals to detach from worldly attachments, desires, and distractions. By letting go of mundane concerns and purifying the mind from excessive desires, individuals can create a mental space that is more receptive to the *divine presence*.

Purification also involves the cleansing of negative emotions, like anger, envy, and greed. These emotions are seen as obstacles that distort the individual's perception and hinder their connection with the divine. By purifying the emotions, individuals can encourage virtues like love, compassion, and humility, which are determined conducive to *divine communion*.

Practices of *purification* in *theurgy* can include self-reflection, self-examination, and the cultivation of ethical conduct. By examining one's thoughts, actions, and intentions, individuals become aware of any harmful tendencies and can *work* towards transforming them. Ethical conduct, like honesty, integrity, and selflessness, is determined essential for establishing a pure and virtuous mindset.

Furthermore, *asceticism*, or *askisi*, is another important aspect of theurgical practice. *Asceticism* involves the disciplined practice of self-control, self-restraint, and renunciation of worldly comforts and indulgences.

It is a means of training the mind and body, disciplining the senses, and redirecting one's energy towards spiritual pursuits.

Ascetic practices in *theurgy* can take various forms, depending on the individual's capacity and inclination. They may include fasting, solitude, silence, simplicity of lifestyle, and moderation in material possessions. By voluntarily renouncing worldly attachments and comforts, individuals free themselves from excessive desires and distractions, allowing them to focus more fully on their spiritual path.

The purpose of *asceticism* in *theurgy* is not self-punishment or denial of pleasure for its own sake. Instead, it is a deliberate choice to simplify one's life and direct one's energy towards spiritual growth and communion with the divine. Ascetic practices help individuals develop inner strength, discipline, and resilience, allowing them to overcome obstacles and temptations that may hinder their spiritual progress.

Asceticism also acts to detach individuals from identification with the body and the material world. By recognizing the impermanence and transitory nature of physical existence, individuals shift their focus towards the eternal and the divine. This detachment enables a deeper exploration of the spiritual realms and nurtures a sense of inner freedom and liberation.

In theurgical practice, *purification* and *asceticism* create the necessary conditions for the individual to approach the divine with sincerity, devotion, and receptivity. The *purification* of the mind and heart allows for clearer perception and a deeper connection with the *divine energies*. Ascetic practices, on the other hand, refine the individual's energy and direct it towards spiritual transformation and union with the divine.

Purification and *asceticism* are closely intertwined with theurgical rituals and practices. Rituals often include acts of *purification*, like the use of water, incense, or sacred objects, which symbolically cleanse the individual and the *ritual* space. These acts of *purification* help create a sacred and consecrated environment conducive to spiritual communion.

The importance of *purification* and *asceticism* in
theurgy is also seen in the concept of "metanoia."
Metanoia, often translated as "spiritual conversion" or
"change of heart," refers to a revelatory transformation
of one's inner being. It involves a shift in consciousness,
values, and priorities, leading to a reorientation towards the divine and the pursuit of spiritual truth.

    Metanoia requires *purification* and ascetic prac-
tices as essential components of the transformative
process. It is through the conscious choice to purify
oneself and engage in ascetic disciplines that individuals
create the conditions for *metanoia* to occur. The practice
of *purification* and *asceticism* clears the path for spiritual
growth and paves the way for the individual to participate fully in the theurgic process.

    In culmination, *purification* and *asceticism* hold
significant importance in *theurgical practices*. *Purification*
involves the removal of impurities, distractions, and
negative influences that hinder spiritual progress. It
creates a state of inner clarity, receptivity, and harmony, allowing individuals to approach the divine with a

purified intention and an open heart. *Asceticism,* on the other hand, involves the disciplined practice of self-control, self-restraint, and renunciation of worldly comforts and indulgences. It redirects one's energy towards spiritual pursuits, encouraging inner strength, discipline, and resilience. Together, *purification* and *asceticism* create the necessary conditions for individuals to approach the divine with sincerity, devotion, and receptivity, facilitating spiritual growth, transformation, and union with the divine.

VI: INVOCATION OF DEITIES AND ANGELS

The *invocation* of *deities* and *angels* is a central aspect of theurgical rituals in various mystical traditions, including Neoplatonic *theurgy*. The act of invoking *divine beings* involves calling upon their presence, power, and guidance during the ritualistic practices. In Greek, the term for *invocation* is "επίκληση" (*epíklisi*), and the term for *deity* is "θεότητα" (*theótita*), while *angels* are referred to as "άγγελοι" (*ángeloi*) in Greek.

In *theurgy*, the *invocation* of *deities* and *angels* serves several purposes. Firstly, it establishes a direct and personal connection between the practitioner and the *divine beings* being invoked. By invoking specific *deities* or *angels*, practitioners seek their presence, blessings, and assistance in their spiritual quest.

The *invocation* of *deities* and *angels* also allows for the participation in their *divine energies* and activities. Through the act of *invocation*, practitioners align themselves with the qualities and attributes of the invoked beings, seeking to absorb their wisdom, power, and transformative qualities.

Moreover, the *invocation* of *deities* and *angels* helps to create a sacred and ritualistic atmosphere during *theurgical practices*. It sets the intention and focus of the *ritual*, creating a space where the practitioner can engage in a deeper level of spiritual communion and receptivity.

In Neoplatonic *theurgy*, the choice of *deities* and *angels* to invoke is often based on their specific qualities, *correspondences*, and associations. Each *deity* or angel stands for certain aspects of reality, divine principles, or cosmic forces. By invoking specific beings, practitioners seek to attune themselves to those particular qualities and establish a deeper connection with them.

For example, the *invocation* of Apollo, the Greek god associated with *music*, *poetry*, and *prophecy*, may be performed to invoke inspiration, creativity, and insight. Similarly, the *invocation* of Hermes, the messenger of the gods, may be performed to invoke communication, guidance, and the power of transitions.

The *invocation* of *deities* and *angels* typically involves the recitation of prayers, invocations, and sacred names. These spoken or chanted words are determined powerful tools to establish a direct connection with the *divine beings*. They carry vibrational energy, sacred intent, and serve as vehicles for communication with the invoked beings.

The prayers and invocations used in the *invocation* of *deities* and *angels* may be derived from sacred texts, oral traditions, or personal inspiration. They often express reverence, gratitude, and requests for divine assistance, guidance, and blessings.

In addition to prayers and invocations, the use of sacred names is also prominent in the *invocation* of *deities* and *angels*. Sacred names are believed to encapsulate the essence and power of the invoked beings. By uttering these names, practitioners seek to establish a direct link with the *divine beings* and tap into their *divine qualities* and energies.

The use of symbolic objects and gestures is often employed during the *invocation* of *deities* and *angels* as well. Objects like *talismans*, *amulets*, or representations of *deities* and *angels* are used as focal points for concentration and connection. They serve as intermediaries between the practitioner and the invoked beings, helping to establish a tangible and visual connection.

Gestures like raising the hands in supplication, bowing, or prostrating can also accompany the *invocation* of *deities* and *angels*. These physical actions symbolize reverence, surrender, and openness to the *divine presence*. They help to align the practitioner's body, mind, and spirit with the energies and qualities of the invoked beings.

The timing and sequencing of the *invocation* of *deities* and *angels* may also be significant in theurgical rituals. Certain celestial alignments, planetary hours, or specific dates may be determined more auspicious for invoking specific *divine beings*. These temporal aspects are believed to enhance the resonance with the invoked forces and create a deeper connection.

It is important to note that the *invocation* of *deities* and *angels* in theurgical rituals is approached with reverence, respect, and a genuine desire for communion with the divine. The intention behind the *invocation* is to establish a sacred and participatory connection, seeking guidance, wisdom, and transformation from the invoked beings.

Furthermore, the *invocation* of *deities* and *angels* in theurgical rituals should not be seen as an attempt to control or manipulate *divine forces* for personal gain. It is an act of devotion, surrender, and opening oneself to the higher realms of existence. The practitioner acknowledges the presence and power of the *divine beings* and seeks to align themselves with their *divine will* and purpose.

In culmination, the *invocation* of *deities* and *angels* is a central aspect of theurgical rituals in various mystical traditions, including Neoplatonic *theurgy*. It establishes a direct connection between the practitioner and the invoked beings, enabling the practitioner to participate in their *divine energies* and activities. Through the recitation of prayers, invocations, and sacred names, practitioners seek the presence, guidance, and blessings of the invoked beings. The use of symbolic objects, gestures, and timing enhances the ritualistic atmosphere and deepens the connection with the invoked forces. The *invocation* of *deities* and *angels* is approached with reverence, respect, and a sincere desire for communion with the divine, allowing practitioners to tap into higher realms of existence and experience transformative spiritual experiences.

VII: THEURGY AND ASTROLOGY

The relationship between *theurgy* and *astrology* is a significant aspect of mystical traditions, including Neoplatonic *theurgy*. *Astrology*, the study of celestial bodies and their influence on human affairs, holds an important place in *theurgical practices*. In Greek, the term for *astrology* is "αστρολογία" (astrología), and the term for *theurgy* is "θεουργία" (*Theourgia*).

Astrology provides a scaffolding for understanding the enmeshment between the celestial realms and the human world. It recognizes the influence of the planets, stars, and other celestial bodies on human life and events. This understanding is important in *theurgy* as it helps practitioners attune themselves to cosmic rhythms, energies, and influences.

Theurgy recognizes the inherent connection between the macrocosm (the universe) and the microcosm (the individual). It acknowledges that celestial forces and energies can be harnessed and utilized in spiritual practices to facilitate the ascent of the soul towards the divine.

One of the key principles in the relationship between *theurgy* and *astrology* is the concept of "*sympathy*" or "*correspondence*." This principle states that there is a *correspondence* or resonance between the celestial world and the earthly world. The movements and positions of celestial bodies are seen as reflecting and influencing events and qualities in the terrestrial world.

Astrology provides a symbolic language through which *theurgy* can interpret and *work* with these *correspondences*. Celestial bodies, zodiac signs, planetary aspects, and other astrological factors are determined to embody specific energies, archetypal qualities, and spiritual principles. *Theurgy* utilizes this symbolic language to align with and invoke these energies during spiritual practices.

In *theurgy*, *astrology* is employed in various ways. One of the primary uses of *astrology* is in the timing of theurgical rituals and practices. Celestial alignments, planetary hours, and specific astrological configurations are determined when determining the most auspicious times for the performance of rituals or spiritual activities.

For example, *theurgical practices* may be scheduled to coincide with favorable planetary aspects or specific zodiacal influences. These celestial alignments are believed to amplify the energies and facilitate a deeper connection with the *divine realms*.

Astrology also provides guidance for the selection of *symbols*, rituals, and invocations in *theurgical practices*. The *correspondences* between celestial bodies and various aspects of life are utilized to choose the appropriate *symbols*, invocations, and rituals that align with the intended spiritual aims.

For instance, the planetary *correspondences* can be used to determine which *deities* or angelic beings to invoke in a specific *ritual*. Each planet is associated with certain qualities, attributes, and energies, and by invoking the corresponding beings, practitioners can align themselves with those particular energies.

Moreover, *astrology* is employed in *theurgical practices* to enhance self-understanding and spiritual growth. The natal chart, which is a map of the positions of celestial bodies at the time of an individual's birth, is used as a tool for self-reflection and self-awareness.

The natal chart provides insights into an individual's personality traits, strengths, weaknesses, and life lessons. By understanding the astrological influences at play, individuals can gain a deeper understanding of themselves and their spiritual path. This self-awareness can inform *theurgical practices* and help individuals align their intentions and efforts with their cosmic blueprint.

Astrology is also used in *theurgical practices* to navigate spiritual progress and personal transformation. *Transit astrology*, which involves analyzing the movement of celestial bodies in relation to an individual's natal chart, provides guidance on the timing and nature of significant life events and spiritual developments.

By understanding the astrological influences at specific periods, individuals can align their efforts and spiritual practices accordingly. They can choose to engage in specific rituals, practices, or meditations that correspond to the energies at play, thereby maximizing their potential for growth and transformation.

Furthermore, *astrology* is employed in *theurgy* to encourage a deeper connection with the *celestial intelligences*. These intelligences are believed to govern and guide the movements of celestial bodies and the unfolding of cosmic events. By attuning oneself to these intelligences, individuals can establish a deeper connection with the cosmic order and participate more fully in the divine plan.

Astrological *talismans* and *amulets* are also utilized in *theurgical practices*. These objects are created in accordance with specific astrological configurations and are believed to harness and amplify the energies associated with those configurations. By wearing or using these *talismans*, individuals can align themselves with the desired planetary or celestial influences.

It is important to note that the relationship between *theurgy* and *astrology* is not deterministic. *Theurgical practices* realize the potential for free will and the ability of individuals to co-create their reality. While *astrology* provides insights and guidance, it is ultimately up to the individual to engage in the spiritual practices and make choices aligned with their spiritual aspirations.

In culmination, the relationship between *theurgy* and *astrology* is a significant aspect of mystical traditions, including Neoplatonic *theurgy*. *Astrology* provides a scaffolding for understanding the enmeshment between the celestial and terrestrial realms. It offers a symbolic language to interpret cosmic *correspondences* and utilize celestial energies in *theurgical practices*. *Astrology* is employed in the timing of rituals, selection of *symbols* and invocations, self-understanding, and spiritual growth. It helps practitioners align themselves with celestial forces and participate in the cosmic order. By integrating *astrology* into *theurgical practices*, individuals can deepen their connection with the divine and align themselves with the cosmic rhythms that underlie spiritual transformation.

VIII: TALISMANS AND AMULETS

The use of *talismans* and *amulets* is a significant aspect of *theurgical practices* in various mystical traditions, including Neoplatonic *theurgy*. *Talismans* and *amulets* are believed to harness and amplify specific energies, qualities, and spiritual intentions, thereby facilitating the practitioner's connection with the divine. In Greek, the term for *talisman* is "ταλισμάνι" (*talismaní*), and the term for *amulet* is "αμουλέτα" (*amouléta*).

Talismans and *amulets* are objects imbued with symbolic importance and charged with specific intentions and energies. They act as intermediaries between the human world and the celestial or *divine realms*, helping to establish a tangible connection with the desired forces or beings.

The use of *talismans* and *amulets* in *theurgical practices* serve a few purposes. Firstly, they are employed as tools to focus and direct intention. The process of creating or consecrating a *talisman* or *amulet* involves imbuing it with specific intentions and aligning it with the desired energies or beings. By holding or wearing the *talisman* or *amulet*, practitioners can continually remind themselves of their spiritual goals and intentions, thus strengthening their focus and commitment.

Secondly, *talismans* and *amulets* are believed to enhance the practitioner's connection with specific celestial or *divine forces*. They act as receptacles or containers for those energies, making them more accessible to the practitioner. The *talisman* or *amulet* is believed to vibe with and amplify the desired energies, thereby facilitating a deeper connection and participation in the desired spiritual qualities or intentions.

The process of creating or consecrating *talismans* and *amulets* in *theurgical practices* often involves rituals and ceremonies. These rituals infuse the objects with sacred intent and divine blessings, thereby enhancing their potency. The rituals may include the recitation of prayers, invocations, the use of specific gestures, or the exposure of the object to sacred elements like incense, blessed water, or consecrated objects.

The selection of materials, *symbols*, and designs for *talismans* and *amulets* is significant. Each material, *symbol*, or design is chosen based on its *correspondence* to specific energies, qualities, or intentions. For example, gemstones may be selected based on their color, vibrational properties, or planetary associations. *Symbols* like sacred geometry, planetary sigils, or divine names may also be incorporated into the design of the *talisman* or *amulet*.

The purpose of the *talisman* or *amulet* determines its specific design and composition. For instance, a *talisman* intended for protection may incorporate *symbols* associated with spiritual defense or warding off negative influences. A *talisman* aimed at enhancing spiritual insight and intuition may incorporate *symbols* associated with the third eye or higher spiritual faculties.

The wearing or carrying of *talismans* and *amulets* during *theurgical practices* acts as a reminder and an embodiment of the practitioner's spiritual intentions and aspirations. It helps to maintain a conscious connection with the desired energies or beings throughout the practice. *Talismans* and *amulets* can be worn as jewelry, carried in a pocket or pouch, or placed on an altar or sacred space.

The efficacy of *talismans* and *amulets* in *theurgical practices* is believed to stem from the principle of sympathetic resonance. This principle suggests that objects or *symbols* infused with specific energies or intentions can vibe with and attract similar energies or influences. The *talisman* or *amulet* acts as a conduit, aligning the practitioner's energy and consciousness with the desired spiritual qualities or intentions.

It is important to note that the use of *talismans* and *amulets* in *theurgical practices* is not based on blind faith or superstition. The efficacy of *talismans* and *amulets* is believed to lie in the practitioner's conscious intention, focus, and alignment with the divine. The objects themselves serve as reminders and anchors for the practitioner's spiritual aspirations, enhancing their commitment and connection to the desired energies or beings.

The selection, consecration, and use of *talismans* and *amulets* in *theurgical practices* are individual and subjective processes. Practitioners may choose to create their own *talismans* or *amulets*, incorporating *symbols* and materials that vibe with their personal spiritual path and intentions. Alternatively, they may acquire *talismans* or *amulets* that are created by skilled practitioners or artisans specifically for the desired purpose.

In Neoplatonic *theurgy*, *talismans* and *amulets* can be used to align with specific celestial forces or intelligences. Each celestial body is associated with certain qualities, energies, and intelligences. By choosing a *talisman* or *amulet* corresponding to a specific celestial body, practitioners seek to align themselves with the energies and qualities associated with that celestial influence.

For example, a *talisman* or *amulet* associated with the Sun may be used to invoke qualities like vitality, creativity, and illumination. A *talisman* or *amulet* associated with the Moon may be used to enhance intuition, emotional balance, and receptivity. By wearing or carrying these *talismans* or *amulets*, practitioners seek to align themselves with and embody these celestial energies.

In culmination, the use of *talismans* and *amulets* is a significant aspect of *theurgical practices* in various mystical traditions, including Neoplatonic *theurgy*. *Talismans* and *amulets* serve as tools to focus intention, enhance connection with specific celestial or *divine forces*, and align with desired energies or qualities. They are created or consecrated with specific intentions, *symbols*, and designs, and their use helps practitioners maintain a conscious connection with their spiritual aspirations. *Talismans* and *amulets* are based on the principle of sympathetic resonance, and their efficacy is believed to lie in the practitioner's intention, focus, and alignment with the divine. By incorporating *talismans* and *amulets* into *theurgical practices*, individuals can deepen their connection with the desired spiritual qualities or intentions and enhance their participation in the divine plan.

IX: Divination and Prophecy

Theurgical techniques for *divination* and *prophecy* are integral aspects of mystical traditions, including Neoplatonic *theurgy*. *Divination* and *prophecy* involve the process of seeking insight, guidance, and knowledge about the past, present, and future through spiritual means. In Greek, the term for *divination* is "μαντεία" (*manteía*), and the term for *prophecy* is "προφητεία" (*propheteía*).

Theurgy utilizes specific techniques to access higher realms of consciousness and receive divine messages and insights. These techniques are aimed at attuning the practitioner's awareness to the spiritual dimensions and allowing for the reception of *divine wisdom* and knowledge. Theurgical *divination* and *prophecy* serve as tools for spiritual guidance, self-discovery, and aligning one's actions with the *divine will*.

One of the primary techniques for *divination* and *prophecy* in *theurgy* is the practice of *oracles*. *Oracles* are individuals who serve as intermediaries between the *divine world* and the human world, providing insights, messages, and guidance from higher intelligences. The oracular process often involves entering into altered states of consciousness through *meditation*, rituals, or other spiritual practices.

The oracular techniques employed in *theurgy* can vary, depending on the tradition and the individual practitioner. Some techniques involve the use of specific tools or objects, like scrying mirrors, crystal balls, or Tarot cards. Others rely on direct communication with *divine beings* through inner visionary experiences or auditory perceptions.

The purpose of the oracular process in *theurgy* is to receive guidance, answers to specific questions, or insights into one's spiritual path and life circumstances. The oracular messages are believed to come from higher intelligences, celestial forces, or *divine beings* who possess a broader perspective and knowledge of the cosmic order.

Another technique for *divination* and *prophecy* in *theurgy* is the interpretation of omens and signs. Omens and signs are believed to be messages from the *divine world*, revealing insights and guidance about future

events or the alignment of energies. Practitioners of
theurgy develop the ability to discern and interpret these
signs, which can manifest through various channels
like dreams, synchronicities, or encounters with ani-
mals.

The interpretation of omens and signs in theurgical *divination* involves a deep understanding of symbolism, *correspondences*, and archetypal patterns. Practitioners learn to realize patterns and connections between the symbolic language of the divine and the
events unfolding in the earthly world.

Astrological *divination* is another technique employed in *theurgy*. *Astrology* is utilized to gain insights
into the influences and energies at play in an individual's life or specific events. The practitioner examines
celestial configurations, planetary aspects, and other
astrological factors to discern the patterns and potential
outcomes.

By understanding the astrological influences,
practitioners can offer guidance and predictions regarding various aspects of life, including relationships,

career, health, and spiritual development. Astrological *divination* provides a scaffolding for understanding the relationship between celestial forces and the individual's life circumstances.

Dream interpretation is also utilized as a technique for *divination* and *prophecy* in *theurgy*. Dreams are seen as a window into the subconscious mind and the spiritual realms. The interpretation of dreams involves discerning the symbolic language used by the unconscious and the divine to communicate messages and insights.

Theurgical practitioners pay close attention to dream *symbols*, themes, and emotions, seeking patterns and connections that offer guidance and deeper understanding. Dreams may provide insights into unresolved issues, hidden potentials, or upcoming challenges. The interpretation of dreams requires a combination of intuition, knowledge of symbolism, and personal understanding of the dreamer's unique circumstances.

In addition to specific techniques, theurgical *divination* and *prophecy* require the cultivation of certain qualities and states of consciousness. These include heightened awareness, receptivity, and attunement to the subtle energies and messages from the *divine realms*. The practitioner develops the ability to quiet the mind, open the heart, and listen deeply to the promptings of the divine within.

The ethical and moral dimension is also integral to theurgical *divination* and *prophecy*. Practitioners approach *divination* with a sense of responsibility, integrity, and respect for the *divine forces* involved. They strive to align their intentions with the highest good and avoid using *divination* for personal gain or manipulation.

It is important to note that theurgical *divination* and *prophecy* are not deterministic. The insights and guidance received through these techniques are subject to interpretation and may be influenced by the individual's choices and actions. *Theurgy* recognizes the potential for free will and the ability of individuals to co-create their reality.

In culmination, theurgical techniques for *divination* and *prophecy* are essential aspects of mystical traditions, including Neoplatonic *theurgy*. These techniques involve accessing higher realms of consciousness, receiving divine messages and insights, and aligning one's actions with the *divine will*. Theurgical *divination* and *prophecy* utilize *oracles*, interpretation of omens and signs, astrological *divination*, and dream interpretation to gain insights and guidance about the past, present, and future. These techniques require receptivity, attunement, and ethical considerations. By engaging in theurgical *divination* and *prophecy*, individuals can seek spiritual guidance, self-discovery, and alignment with the divine purpose.

X: THE SOUL'S QUEST THROUGH DIFFERENT REALMS

Theurgy and the concept of the *soul's quest* through different realms are interconnected aspects of mystical traditions, including Neoplatonic *theurgy*. The concept of the *soul's quest* involves the understanding that the soul progresses and evolves through various levels of existence, ultimately seeking union with the divine. In Greek, the term for the soul is "ψυχή" (*psychē*), and the term for quest is "ταξίδι" (*taxídi*).

According to the concept of the *soul's quest* in *theurgy*, the soul is seen as a divine spark or emanation from the *divine source*. It embarks on a transformative quest, experiencing different realms and states of consciousness while seeking to reunite with its *divine origin*. This quest is often described as a return to the divine, a process of awakening and remembering its true nature.

Theurgy recognizes multiple levels or realms of existence, each with its own characteristics, energies, and *divine intelligences*. These realms are seen as interconnected and interpenetrating, forming a multidimensional reality. The *soul's quest* involves traversing and experiencing these realms as it evolves and grows in spiritual understanding.

The first world in the *soul's quest* is often associated with the physical world, the world of matter and embodiment. In this world, the soul experiences the bounds and challenges of physical existence. It interacts with the material world and undergoes various life experiences, which serve as opportunities for growth, learning, and self-realization.

The physical world is regarded as a necessary and meaningful part of the *soul's quest*. It provides a platform for the soul to develop virtues, overcome obstacles, and acquire the experiences needed for its spiritual evolution. *Theurgical practices* often incorporate techniques for cultivating awareness, mindfulness, and spiritual growth within the context of physical existence.

As the soul progresses in its quest, it may ascend to higher realms of consciousness and existence. These realms are often described as more refined and subtle than the physical world, with increased access to *divine energies* and intelligences. The quest through these realms involves the refinement and expansion of the soul's consciousness, allowing for deeper insights, spiritual communion, and transformative experiences.

In Neoplatonic *theurgy*, the concept of the *soul's quest* is often described in terms of ascending through the various levels of the *cosmic hierarchy*. This *hierarchy* is believed to consist of different levels or spheres of reality, each governed by *divine intelligences* or principles. The *soul's quest* involves transcending the bounds of each level and ascending to higher levels of consciousness and spiritual realization.

For example, in the Neoplatonic tradition, the soul is believed to ascend through the realms associated with the celestial bodies, like the Moon, the planets, and the stars. Each celestial world is associated with specific qualities, energies, and *divine intelligences*. By ascending through these celestial realms, the soul acquires the corresponding qualities and experiences the *divine presence* associated with each world.

Theurgical practices facilitate the soul's quest through different realms by providing techniques for spiritual transformation, elevation of consciousness, and communion with *divine energies*. These practices involve *purification, meditation, invocation, contemplation,* and other spiritual disciplines that refine the soul's awareness and align it with the divine.

Purification is a key aspect of *theurgical practices* in relation to the *soul's quest*. *Purification* involves the removal of impurities, attachments, and bounds that hinder the soul's progress. It allows the soul to disentangle itself from the distractions and entrapments of the lower realms, facilitating its ascent to higher levels of consciousness.

Meditation and *contemplation* are also integral to the *soul's quest* in *theurgy*. These practices enable the soul to go beyond the bounds of ordinary consciousness and enter into higher states of awareness. Through *meditation* and *contemplation*, the soul can commune with the *divine intelligences*, receive insights and guidance, and experience transformative states of consciousness.

Invocation is another important aspect of *theur-gical practices* in relation to the *soul's quest*. By invoking specific *deities*, angelic beings, or *divine energies*, the soul establishes a connection and rapport with the higher realms. The *invocation* allows the soul to receive guid-ance, inspiration, and divine blessings that facilitate its spiritual growth and progress.

In addition to ascending through different realms, the *soul's quest* in *theurgy* also involves the process of unification and reunion with the divine. The ultimate aim of the *soul's quest* is to go beyond all bounds, merge with the *divine source*, and attain a state of union or oneness. This state of union is often de-scribed as a return to the *divine origin*, a realization of the soul's inherent divinity.

Theurgical practices provide tools and techniques for facilitating the *soul's quest* towards union with the divine. Through the practices of *contemplation, invocation, purification,* and other spiritual disciplines, the soul gradually aligns itself with the *divine will,* wisdom, and presence. It sheds the bounds and illusions of separate existence and experiences a revelatory sense of unity, wholeness, and *transcendence*.

It is important to note that the concept of the *soul's quest* in *theurgy* is not linear or sequential in a strict sense. The *soul's quest* is often described as a multidimensional and nonlinear process, with the soul simultaneously experiencing and exploring different realms and levels of consciousness. The stages of the *soul's quest* are not fixed, and individuals may have unique experiences and paths based on their spiritual development and evolutionary needs.

In culmination, *theurgy* recognizes the concept of the *soul's quest* through different realms as an integral aspect of mystical traditions. The *soul's quest* involves traversing and experiencing various levels of existence, seeking spiritual growth, and ultimately striving for union with the divine. *Theurgical practices* facilitate this quest through techniques of *purification, meditation, invocation*, and other spiritual disciplines. By engaging in these practices, individuals can awaken to their true nature, expand their consciousness, and participate in the divine plan of the soul's evolution.

XI: THEURGY-BREATHED ART AND ARCHITECTURE

Theurgy and *theurgy*-breathed *art* and *architecture* are interconnected aspects of mystical traditions, including Neoplatonic *theurgy*. *Theurgy*, in its essence, is the practice of engaging with the divine and facilitating spiritual transformation. In Greek, the term for *art* is "τέχνη" (*téchnē*), and the term for *architecture* is "αρχιτεκτονική" (*architektoniki*).

Theurgy-breathed *art* and *architecture* serve as powerful expressions of the mystical and spiritual dimensions of *theurgical practices*. They provide visual and spatial representations of the divine, evoke transcendent experiences, and create sacred environments for spiritual communion and transformation.

Theurgy-breathed *art* includes various forms, including painting, sculpture, iconography, and sacred *symbols*. These artistic expressions aim to convey the qualities, energies, and archetypal principles associated with the *divine realms*. The *art* acts as a means of *contemplation*, inspiration, and deepening of the spiritual connection.

In Neoplatonic *theurgy*, *art* is seen as a medium through which the divine is made manifest in the physical world. Artists are regarded as channels or vessels for the *divine inspiration*, translating higher truths and realities into tangible forms. The creation of *art* becomes a sacred act, a means of invoking the *divine presence* and sharing its beauty and wisdom with others.

Theurgical *art* often incorporates symbolic language and imagery that stands for spiritual concepts, cosmic forces, and *divine beings*. These *symbols* serve as portals to deeper realms of consciousness, inviting viewers to contemplate and connect with the *divine qualities* they represent.

For example, in Christian *theurgy*, iconography holds a significant place. *Icons* are determined windows into the *divine world*, serving as visual representations of saints, *angels*, and the *divine presence*. *Icons* are believed to embody the energies and qualities of the depicted beings, and through *contemplation* and veneration, viewers can establish a direct connection with the divine.

Similarly, sacred *symbols* like mandalas, yantras, or sacred geometry are used in theurgical *art*. These *symbols* are created based on precise geometric patterns and are believed to hold transformative and harmonizing energies. They act as visual focal points for *meditation*, concentration, and spiritual alignment.

The use of color is also significant in theurgical *art*. Different colors are associated with specific energies, qualities, and states of consciousness. Artists may utilize specific color schemes to evoke certain moods, spiritual states, or to represent particular divine principles. The colors employed in theurgical *art* can amplify the vibrational effect of the artwork and create a deeper resonance with the viewer.

Moreover, theurgical *art* often seeks to evoke a sense of *transcendence*, beauty, and awe. The use of harmonious proportions, graceful forms, and skillful craftsmanship wants to uplift the viewer and awaken a sense of the divine within. The artistic creation becomes a transformative experience for both the artist and the viewer, allowing for a deeper connection with the spiritual dimensions.

In addition to *art, theurgy*-breathed *architecture* holds a significant place in creating sacred spaces and environments conducive to spiritual practices and experiences. The design and layout of sacred buildings and temples are carefully planned to align with the principles of harmony, symbolism, and energetic resonance.

In Neoplatonic *theurgy, architecture* is seen as a manifestation of the cosmic order and a reflection of the *divine harmony*. Sacred *architecture* incorporates sacred geometry, proportions, and symbolism to create spaces that vibe with the spiritual aspirations of the practitioner. The arrangement of spaces, the use of light and sound, and the choice of materials contribute to the overall transformative experience within the sacred environment.

For example, in ancient Greece, the temples committed to the gods were designed according to specific architectural principles. The use of the golden ra-

tio, precise measurements, and sacred geometrical proportions aimed to create spaces that harmonized with
the *divine order* and facilitated spiritual communion.

In Christian *theurgy*, cathedral *architecture* is
often breathed by the desire to create spaces that evoke
a sense of awe, *transcendence*, and spiritual ascent.
Cathedrals are designed with soaring ceilings, complex
stained glass windows, and labyrinthine layouts that
invite *contemplation*, prayer, and connection with the
divine.

Theurgical *architecture* also incorporates the use
of sacred *symbols*, like mandalas or cosmic diagrams,
within the design of the sacred spaces. These *symbols* are
integrated into the architectural elements, like domes,
arches, or altars, serving as visual reminders of the *divine presence* and the spiritual quest.

Furthermore, theurgical *architecture* often pays
attention to the relationship between light and shadow.
Natural light is utilized to create a sense of illumination
and spiritual upliftment. The use of stained glass windows, skylights, or specific openings allows light to fil-

ter into the sacred space, creating a mystical ambiance and evoking a sense of *divine presence*.

Acoustic considerations also play a place in theurgical *architecture*. The design and construction of sacred spaces take into account the acoustics and sound vibrations, creating environments conducive to chant, prayer, or meditative practices. The careful arrangement of spaces and materials allows for enhanced sound resonance, encouraging a deeper connection with the divine through sound.

Theurgical-breathed *art* and *architecture* have the power to transform the viewer or participant's consciousness, creating a sacred and transformative experience. By engaging with the symbolism, beauty, and spatial qualities of the artwork or *architecture*, individuals can deepen their spiritual connection, evoke transcendent states of consciousness, and align themselves with the divine.

In culmination, *theurgy*-breathed *art* and *architecture* are powerful expressions of the mystical and spiritual dimensions of *theurgical practices*. They convey the qualities and energies associated with the *divine realms*, create sacred environments for spiritual communion, and evoke transformative experiences. Theurgical *art* employs symbolism, sacred *symbols*, and skillful craftsmanship to inspirit *contemplation*, connection, and spiritual growth. Theurgical *architecture* incorporates sacred geometry, proportions, and symbolic elements to create sacred spaces conducive to spiritual practices and experiences. By engaging with *theurgy*-breathed *art* and *architecture*, individuals can deepen their spiritual connection, evoke transcendent states of consciousness, and participate in the transformative quest towards the divine.

XII: Divine Emanation

Theurgy and the concept of *divine emanation* are intimately connected within mystical traditions, including Neoplatonic *theurgy*. *Divine emanation* refers to the process through which the *divine essence* or energies flow forth from the ultimate source and manifest in various levels of reality. In Greek, the term for *divine emanation* is "θεία εκπομπή" (theía ekpompí).

The concept of *divine emanation* is ineradicable from the understanding that the ultimate reality or *divine source* is beyond human comprehension and goes beyond all bounds. The divine is seen as infinite, eternal, and beyond any form or definition. However, the divine is also determined to be immanent, pervading and animating all aspects of existence.

Theurgy recognizes that the *divine essence* manifests and unfolds itself in a hierarchical manner, with each level or world emanating from *the one* preceding it. This hierarchical structure is often referred to as the "*Great Chain of Being*" or the "*cosmic hierarchy*." It stands for a continuum of existence, ranging from the most subtle and transcendent realms to the most material and tangible forms.

According to the concept of *divine emanation* in *theurgy*, the ultimate source, often referred to as the "One" or the "Good," emanates or radiates its *divine energies* and qualities. These emanations flow forth in a cascading manner, creating various levels of reality or planes of existence.

The first emanation from the *divine source* is often described as the "*Nous*" or "*Intellect*." The *Nous* stands for the highest level of *divine intelligence*, encompassing perfect knowledge, wisdom, and understanding. It is the world of pure thought and the source of all ideas and archetypes. The *Nous* acts as the intermediary between the *divine source* and the following levels of manifestation.

From the *Nous*, further emanations occur, giving rise to the world of the "*World Soul*" or "*Anima Mundi*." The *World Soul* is the cosmic soul that permeates and animates the entire physical universe. It is the intermediary between the higher realms and the material world, serving as the link between the divine and the earthly.

The *World Soul* is associated with the principles of life, vitality, and harmony. It governs the cycles of nature, the movements of celestial bodies, and the unfolding of cosmic events. *Theurgy* recognizes the *World Soul* as the bridge between the transcendent and the immanent, providing a means of accessing *divine energies* and participating in the cosmic order.

The concept of *divine emanation* in *theurgy* extends to the material world as well. The material world, including the physical bodies and all forms of matter, is determined to be an emanation from the *World Soul*. It is the most dense and limited aspect of existence, yet it still carries the imprint of the *divine essence*.

In *theurgy*, the process of spiritual ascent and transformation involves aligning oneself with the *divine energies* and qualities that have emanated through the various levels of reality. *Theurgy* seeks to reconnect individuals with their divine nature and assist them in reuniting with the source from which they have emanated.

Theurgical practices aim to awaken and activate the divine spark within individuals, allowing them to become more conscious of their inherent divinity. By cultivating virtues, purifying the soul, and engaging in spiritual practices, individuals can align themselves with the higher levels of the *cosmic hierarchy* and participate in the divine plan.

Theurgy recognizes that each individual is a unique manifestation of the *divine essence*, carrying a specific purpose and potential. The *divine energies* that have emanated through the *cosmic hierarchy* are believed to be imprinted within each individual's soul. Through spiritual practices, individuals can awaken and actualize these *divine energies*, bringing them into conscious awareness and expression.

Theurgy also acknowledges the existence of *divine intelligences* or beings that reside in the higher realms of the *cosmic hierarchy*. These beings, often referred to as *angels*, *archangels*, or *celestial intelligences*, are determined to be intermediaries between the divine and the human world. They embody specific qualities, energies, and *divine purposes*.

In *theurgical practices*, individuals may invoke and communicate with these *celestial intelligences*, seeking their guidance, blessings, and assistance in their spiritual quest. By establishing a connection and rapport with these *divine beings*, individuals can align themselves more closely with the *divine qualities* they embody and receive their support in their spiritual endeavors.

The concept of *divine emanation* in *theurgy* highlights the inherent unity and enmeshment of all levels of existence. It recognizes that each level of reality, starting with the transcendent to the material, is intimately linked and participates in the *divine order*. *Theurgy* encourages individuals to perceive the *divine presence* in all aspects of existence and to encourage a sense of reverence and awe for the intercollective nexus of life.

In culmination, *theurgy* and the concept of *divine emanation* are intricately intertwined within mystical traditions. *Divine emanation* refers to the process through which the *divine essence* or energies flow forth from the ultimate source and manifest in various levels of reality. *Theurgy* recognizes the hierarchical structure of the cosmic order, with each level emanating from *the one* preceding it. *Theurgy* seeks to awaken individuals to their divine nature, align them with the *divine energies*, and facilitate their quest back to the source from which they have emanated. By participating in *theurgy*, individuals can reconnect with their inherent divinity, perceive the *divine presence* in all aspects of existence, and play an active place in the unfolding of the cosmic plan.

XIII: Theurgical Practices in Late Antique and Byzantine Christianity

Theurgical practices in late antique and Byzantine Christianity refer to the mystical and spiritual practices aimed at union with the divine and the cultivation of a transformative relationship with God. These practices incorporate various elements, including *contemplation*, prayer, sacraments, *asceticism*, and participation in liturgical rituals. In Greek, the term for *theurgical practices* in Christianity is "θεουργικές πρακτικές" (*theourgikés praktikés*).

Late antique and Byzantine Christianity drew upon the valuable mystical traditions of early Christian mystics, desert fathers, and the teachings of the early church fathers, like Origen, Evagrius Ponticus, and Gregory of Nyssa. *Theurgical practices* in Christianity aimed to facilitate a direct and experiential encounter with the divine, leading to spiritual transformation and union with God.

One of the foundational *theurgical practices* in late antique and Byzantine Christianity is *contemplation*. *Contemplation* involves the stilling of the mind, surrendering of the ego, and opening oneself to the presence and *action* of God. It is a receptive practice that allows individuals to enter into a state of deep communion with the divine, transcending the bounds of ordinary consciousness.

Contemplation is often accompanied by the repetition of the *Jesus Prayer*, a short prayer that focuses the mind and heart on the name of Jesus. The *Jesus Prayer* is recited with humility and devotion, inviting the presence of Christ and invoking his grace and mercy. Through the repetition of the prayer, individuals seek to attune themselves to the *divine presence* and experience the transformative power of God's love.

Another significant theurgical practice in late antique and Byzantine Christianity is participation in the sacraments. The sacraments, like baptism, the *Eucharist*, and the sacrament of confession, are determined to be sacred rituals through which individuals encounter the divine and receive the grace of God.

Baptism is seen as the initiation into the Christian faith and the participation in the death and resurrection of Christ. It symbolizes the cleansing and *purifi-*

cation of the soul, preparing the individual for a life of union with God. The *Eucharist,* also known as *Holy Communion,* is the central sacrament of the Christian liturgy, representing the mystical union with the body and blood of Christ.

The sacrament of confession, or repentance, is a theurgical practice that involves the confession of sins, receiving absolution, and seeking reconciliation with God. It is a process of self-examination, humility, and turning away from sinful tendencies, allowing individuals to restore their relationship with God and experience spiritual renewal.

Asceticism is another essential component of *theurgical practices* in late antique and Byzantine Christianity. *Asceticism* involves the disciplined pursuit of virtue, self-control, and detachment from worldly desires. It is a means of purifying the soul, freeing oneself from the distractions of the material world, and sharpening on the pursuit of union with God.

Ascetic practices include fasting, vigils, solitude, and the renunciation of worldly attachments. These practices are undertaken with the intention of subduing the passions, quieting the mind, and cultivating a spirit of detachment and simplicity. By embracing *asceticism*, individuals seek to create inner space for the presence of God and deepen their spiritual connection.

Participation in liturgical rituals is also an integral part of *theurgical practices* in late antique and Byzantine Christianity. The liturgy, or the divine worship, is seen as a sacred act of communion with God and participation in the heavenly world. The liturgical rituals involve specific prayers, chants, hymns, and symbolic actions that create a sacred space and evoke the presence of the divine.

The liturgy is regarded as a transformative experience that allows individuals to enter into the mystical dimensions of time and space. Through active participation in the liturgical rituals, individuals engage in a dynamic encounter with God, participating in the *divine drama* of salvation and receiving the spiritual nourishment needed for their quest towards union with God.

In addition to these practices, late antique and Byzantine Christianity also incorporated the use of *icons* as aids to *contemplation* and spiritual focus. *Icons* are sacred images that depict Christ, the Virgin Mary, saints, and biblical scenes. They are regarded as windows into the *divine world* and serve as focal points for prayer, *meditation*, and spiritual *contemplation*.

Icons are created with careful attention to symbolism, theological accuracy, and artistic beauty. They are believed to radiate the presence and grace of the divine, facilitating the connection between the human and the *divine realms*. The veneration of *icons*, through acts of prayer, kissing, or prostration, is seen as a means of expressing devotion, humility, and reverence for the *divine presence*.

Theurgical practices in late antique and Byzantine Christianity are characterized by a deep reverence for the mystery of God, a commitment to inner transformation, and a desire for intimate communion with the divine. These practices provide a pathway for individuals to experience the transformative power of God's grace and participate in the divine life.

Through *contemplation*, participation in sacraments, *asceticism*, liturgical rituals, and the veneration of *icons*, individuals seek to open themselves to the *divine presence*, purify their souls, and encourage a deep and abiding relationship with God. *Theurgical practices* in late antique and Byzantine Christianity are grounded in the understanding that the divine is immanent, accessible, and actively at *work* in the lives of individuals who seek union with God.

XIV: THEURGY-BREATHED MUSIC AND POETRY

Theurgy and *theurgy*-breathed *music* and *poetry* are interconnected aspects of mystical traditions, including Neoplatonic *theurgy*. *Theurgy*, as the practice of engaging with the divine and facilitating spiritual transformation, finds expression in the realms of *music* and *poetry*. In Greek, the term for *music* is "μουσική" (*mousikē*), and the term for *poetry* is "ποίηση" (poíēsē).

Music and *poetry* have long been recognized as powerful vehicles for connecting with the divine, evoking transcendent experiences, and conveying the ineffable qualities of the mystical realms. *Theurgy*-breathed *music* and *poetry* aim to create sacred and transformative experiences, allowing individuals to deepen their spiritual connection and participate in the *divine presence*.

Music has the ability to move the soul, stir emotions, and go beyond the bounds of ordinary consciousness. The rhythm, melody, harmony, and lyrics of *music* can elicit revelatory responses within individuals, evoking a sense of beauty, awe, and spiritual elevation.

Theurgy-breathed *music* harnesses these qualities to create a sonic territory that vibes with the divine.

In the context of *theurgy*, *music* acts as a means of attuning oneself to the higher frequencies and vibrations of the *divine realms*. *Theurgy*-breathed *music* often incorporates elements like chanting, repetitive melodies, and harmonies that create a meditative and contemplative atmosphere. These musical elements facilitate the opening of the heart, quieting of the mind, and the cultivation of receptivity to the *divine presence*.

Chanting is a significant aspect of *theurgy*-breathed *music*. Chants consist of repetitive vocal phrases or mantras that are sung or recited with intention and devotion. The repetition of sacred sounds or names of the divine is believed to invoke and attune individuals to the energies and qualities associated with the *divine presence*.

Chanting can be done individually or in communal settings, like during religious ceremonies or spiritual gatherings. The rhythmic patterns and melodic structures of the chants create a sense of unity, encouraging a collective experience of shared spirituality and deepening the connection with the divine.

The lyrics of *theurgy*-breathed *music* often contain sacred texts, hymns, or prayers that express devotion, gratitude, and longing for union with the divine. These lyrics serve as vehicles for spiritual *contemplation*, self-reflection, and the expression of revelatory spiritual experiences. The words, when sung or recited with sincerity and intention, can carry the power to transport individuals to higher states of consciousness and evoke a sense of the *divine presence*.

The use of musical instruments also holds a significant place in *theurgy*-breathed *music*. Instruments like the lyre, flute, harp, and drums have been traditionally associated with spiritual and mystical practices. The sounds produced by these instruments create vibrational patterns that vibe with the energetic frequencies of the *divine realms*, further enhancing the transformative power of the *music*.

Similarly, *poetry* has been respected as a form of expression that goes beyond the bounds of ordinary language and conveys deeper truths and insights. The rhythm, imagery, and symbolism of *poetry* can evoke emotions, provoke *contemplation*, and invite individuals into a deeper understanding of the divine mysteries.

Theurgy-breathed *poetry* often employs metaphor, allegory, and symbolic language to convey spiritual truths and experiences. It searches out themes of the *soul's quest*, union with the divine, and the transformative power of love and devotion. The *poetry* invites individuals to contemplate and meditate on the *divine qualities* and to enter into a direct and personal relationship with the divine.

The use of sacred texts, like scriptures or hymns, is common in *theurgy*-breathed *poetry*. These texts serve as sources of inspiration and spiritual guidance, offering insights into the nature of the divine and the path of spiritual transformation. Poets may reinterpret or rephrase the sacred texts, infusing them with personal experiences, emotions, and reflections, creating a bridge between the sacred and the personal.

The language and structure of *theurgy*-breathed *poetry* are often crafted to evoke a sense of beauty, harmony, and spiritual resonance. Poets employ literary techniques like rhythm, rhyme, repetition, and alliteration to create a musicality in the verses, heightening the emotional effect and facilitating a deeper engagement with the divine message.

Theurgy-breathed *music* and *poetry* are not just vehicles for personal expression but also serve as communal practices. They can be performed in group settings, religious ceremonies, or spiritual gatherings, allowing individuals to come together in a shared experience of worship, *contemplation*, and spiritual transformation.

Through *theurgy*-breathed *music* and *poetry*, individuals seek to go beyond the bounds of ordinary existence and enter into the realms of the divine. The combination of musical and poetic elements provides a holistic and multisensory approach to spiritual practice, engaging the mind, body, and soul in the pursuit of union with the divine.

In culmination, *theurgy* and *theurgy*-breathed *music* and *poetry* are interconnected aspects of mystical traditions. *Theurgy*-breathed *music* harnesses the power of sound and rhythm to create a sonic territory that vibes with the divine. Chanting, repetitive melodies, and sacred lyrics invoke the energies and qualities associated with the *divine presence*, facilitating a deeper spiritual connection. *Theurgy*-breathed *poetry* employs symbolism, metaphor, and the beauty of language to convey deeper truths and insights, inviting individuals into a direct and personal relationship with the divine. Through *theurgy*-breathed *music* and *poetry*, individuals seek to go beyond the bounds of ordinary existence, enter into the realms of the divine, and participate in the transformative power of the *divine presence*.

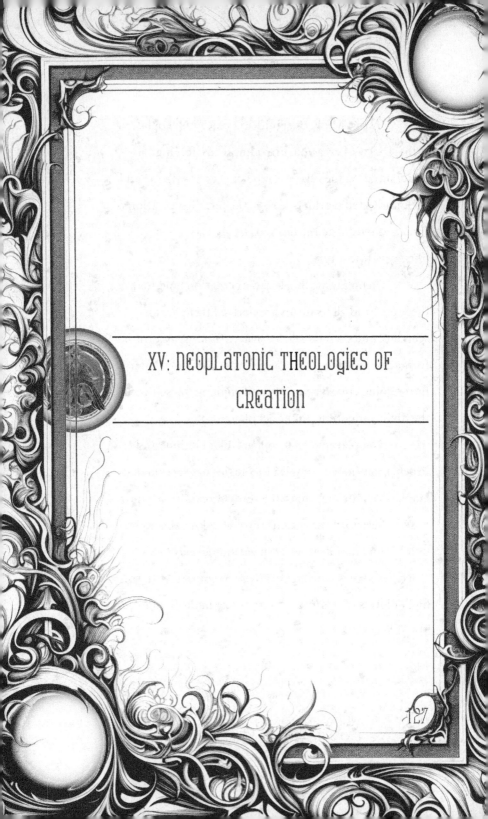

XV: Neoplatonic Theologies of Creation

Theurgy holds a significant place in Neoplatonic theologies of creation, providing a scaffolding for understanding the relationship between the divine and the manifested world. In Greek, the term for creation is "κτίσις" (ktisis), and the term for *theurgy* is "θεουργία" (theourgía).

Neoplatonic theologies of creation hold that the world and all its forms are derived from a transcendent and ineffable *divine source. Theurgy*, as a transformative practice, acts as a means of participating in the ongoing creative process and aligning oneself with the divine intentions in the act of creation.

Neoplatonic philosophers, like Plotinus and Proclus, developed complex theologies of creation that emphasized the hierarchical nature of reality. They proposed a series of emanations through which the divine unfolds and manifests itself in various levels of existence. *Theurgy* is seen as a means to reconnect with the higher levels of reality and participate in the divine creative process.

According to Neoplatonic theologies, the first emanation from the *divine source* is often referred to as the "One" or the "Good." This principle is beyond all categories and attributes, ineffable and transcendent. From *the One*, emanates the "*Nous*" or "*Intellect*," which stands for the world of *divine intelligence* and perfect knowledge. The *Nous* acts as the intermediary between the transcendent One and the following levels of creation.

Theurgy, in this context, is understood as a process of aligning oneself with the *divine intelligence* or the *Nous*. By engaging in *theurgical practices*, individuals seek to elevate their consciousness, purify their souls, and awaken their inherent divine nature. *Theurgy* enables individuals to participate in the divine creative process, realizing their place as co-creators with the divine.

Theurgy is seen as a transformative process that allows individuals to go beyond their limited individuality and merge with the divine consciousness. Through *theurgical practices*, individuals seek to overcome the illusions of separation and realize their inherent unity with the *divine source*. By aligning themselves with the *divine intelligence*, individuals gain access to higher realms of knowledge and participate in the unfolding of the divine plan.

Theurgy in Neoplatonic theologies of creation involves various practices, including *meditation, contemplation, invocation,* and *ritual*. These practices are designed to awaken the divine spark within individuals and encourage a conscious awareness of their connection with the *divine intelligence.*

Meditation and *contemplation* play an important place in *theurgical practices*. By stilling the mind and turning inward, individuals seek to go beyond the bounds of ordinary consciousness and enter into a direct experience of the divine. Through deep *contemplation*, individuals strive to grasp the transcendent realities and gain insight into the divine intentions in the act of creation.

Invocation is another essential aspect of *theurgy* in Neoplatonic theologies of creation. By invoking specific divine names, qualities, or intelligences, individuals establish a connection with the higher realms and attract the corresponding energies and qualities. The *invocation* allows individuals to align themselves with the divine creative powers and participate in the ongoing process of manifestation.

Rituals are also integral to *theurgical practices* in Neoplatonic theologies of creation. Rituals serve as a means of embodying and enacting the transformative intentions in the act of creation. They provide a scaffolding for individuals to engage in symbolic actions, gestures, and ceremonies that align them with the divine principles and energies.

Through *ritual*, individuals create a sacred space and time in which they can commune with the divine and participate in the divine creative process. Rituals often involve the use of sacred objects, gestures, and specific words or incantations that evoke the presence and power of the divine. *Theurgy*-breathed rituals in Neoplatonic theologies of creation aim to facilitate a conscious alignment with the divine intentions and to generate transformative energies.

Theurgy also includes the *purification* of the soul as an essential aspect of the creative process. Neoplatonic theologies emphasize the *purification* of the soul from its attachments, passions, and illusions as a prerequisite for participating in the divine creative process. *Purification* involves the removal of impurities and bounds that hinder the soul's realization of its inherent divine nature.

Through *purification*, individuals strive to refine their consciousness, align their desires with *divine will*, and encourage virtues and qualities associated with the divine. The *purification* of the soul allows individuals to become receptive to the *divine presence*, to vibe with the divine intentions, and to contribute harmoniously to the ongoing creative process.

The place of *theurgy* in Neoplatonic theologies of creation is not just limited to the individual level but also extends to the cosmic level. *Theurgy* is seen as a means of participating in the cosmic order and the harmonious unfolding of creation. Through *theurgical practices*, individuals align themselves with the divine principles that govern the cosmos, contributing to the cosmic harmony and the fulfillment of the divine intentions in the act of creation.

In culmination, *theurgy* holds an important place in Neoplatonic theologies of creation, providing a means of participating in the ongoing creative process and aligning oneself with the divine intentions. *Theurgy* enables individuals to reconnect with the *divine intelligence*, go beyond their limited individuality, and participate in the unfolding of the divine plan. Through practices like *meditation, contemplation, invocation,* and *ritual,* individuals seek to elevate their consciousness, purify their souls, and awaken their inherent divine nature. *Theurgy* is a transformative process that allows individuals to align themselves with the divine principles and energies, contributing to the harmonious unfolding of creation at both the individual and cosmic levels.

XVI: THEURGY-BREATHED PHILOSOPHY

Theurgy and theurgy-breathed philosophy are closely intertwined, as the practice of theurgy often stems from and informs philosophical perspectives. In Greek, the term for philosophy is "φιλοσοφία" (philosophía), and the term for theurgy is "θεουργία" (theourgía).

Theurgy-breathed philosophy is a philosophical approach that recognizes the potential for direct engagement with the divine and the transformative power of this encounter. It acknowledges the bounds of purely rational inquiry and embraces experiential and mystical dimensions of knowledge.

Theurgy-breathed philosophy often emerges within mystical and spiritual traditions that seek to integrate the transcendent and immanent aspects of existence. It draws upon the insights of mystical experiences, spiritual practices, and the contemplation of metaphysical questions to inform its philosophical scaffolding.

One of the key aspects of theurgy-breathed philosophy is the recognition of the divine as the ultimate source and the highest reality. It acknowledges that the nature of the divine is beyond the grasp of rational understanding and goes beyond ordinary concepts and language.

Theurgy-breathed philosophy recognizes that the divine can be encountered through direct experiential means, like *contemplation*, prayer, and participation in spiritual practices. It highlights the importance of personal transformation and the cultivation of virtues as a means to approach and align oneself with the divine.

Theurgy-breathed philosophy often challenges the dualistic separation between the divine and the human, seeking to bridge the gap and promote a sense of unity and enmeshment. It searches out the notion that human beings possess an inherent divine spark and that through spiritual practice, individuals can realize their divine nature and participate in the divine plan.

Theurgy-breathed philosophy recognizes that the pursuit of wisdom and understanding involves not just intellectual inquiry but also a deep engagement with the spiritual dimensions of existence. It highlights the integration of reason and intuition, intellect and emotion, in the quest for knowledge and truth.

One of the central themes in *theurgy*-breathed philosophy is the concept of participation. It acknowledges that individuals are not merely passive observers of reality but active participants in the unfolding of existence. *Theurgy*-breathed philosophy encourages individuals to actively engage with the divine, participate in the creative process, and contribute to the manifestation of higher realities.

The concept of participation extends to the idea that the soul is connected to and influenced by the cosmic order. *Theurgy*-breathed philosophy recognizes the interconnection between the microcosm (the individual) and the macrocosm (the universe), and the ways in which the actions and thoughts of individuals can have a ripple effect on the larger reality.

Theurgy-breathed philosophy often searches out questions related to reality, the purpose of existence, and the meaning of life. It dives into metaphysical inquiries, like the nature of being, the relationship between the physical and spiritual realms, and the nature of consciousness.

Theurgy-breathed philosophy often draws upon symbolism, allegory, and myth to convey deeper truths and insights. It recognizes that language and concepts are limited in capturing the fullness of the divine and the mystical experience. Symbolism and mythic narratives are employed to convey truths that go beyond the confines of rational discourse.

Theurgy-breathed philosophy often promotes a holistic approach to knowledge, recognizing the enmeshment of different disciplines and modes of understanding. It seeks to integrate the insights of philosophy, mysticism, psychology, and other fields of inquiry to develop a comprehensive understanding of the human experience and reality.

Theurgy-breathed philosophy highlights the transformative power of spiritual practices and the cultivation of virtues. It recognizes that philosophical inquiry alone is insufficient to bring about true wisdom and understanding. *Theurgy*-breathed philosophy encourages individuals to engage in spiritual practices, like *meditation, contemplation,* and ethical conduct, to encourage the inner qualities necessary for a deeper engagement with the divine.

Theurgy-breathed philosophy also acknowledges the importance of community and the sharing of wisdom and insights. It recognizes that the spiritual quest is not solely an individual endeavor but is enriched through dialogue, collaboration, and the exchange of ideas with others.

In culmination, *theurgy* and *theurgy*-breathed philosophy are closely intertwined. *Theurgy*-breathed philosophy acknowledges the bounds of rational inquiry and embraces the experiential and mystical dimensions of knowledge. It recognizes the potential for direct engagement with the divine and highlights personal transformation and the cultivation of virtues. *Theurgy*-breathed philosophy searches out questions related to reality, the purpose of existence, and the meaning of life. It promotes a holistic approach to knowledge, drawing upon various disciplines and modes of understanding. *Theurgy*-breathed philosophy encourages individuals to actively participate in the creative process, realize their inherent divine nature, and engage with the spiritual dimensions of existence.

XVII: THEURGY-BREATHED LITERATURE AND DRAMA

Theurgy and *theurgy*-breathed literature and drama are interconnected expressions of mystical and spiritual traditions. They serve as vehicles for exploring and conveying the transformative power of *theurgy* through the medium of storytelling, symbolism, and dramatic representation. In Greek, the term for literature is "λογοτεχνία" (logotechnía) and the term for drama is "δράμα" (drama).

Theurgy-breathed literature and drama utilize narrative, symbolism, and dramatic elements to convey spiritual insights, evoke emotional responses, and invite individuals into a deeper engagement with the divine. These literary and dramatic works draw inspiration from the mystical traditions and incorporate the concepts, themes, and practices associated with *theurgy*.

One of the significant aspects of *theurgy*-breathed literature and drama is the use of symbolism. *Symbols* are employed to represent abstract ideas, spiritual principles, and the divine realities that go beyond ordinary language and concepts. Symbolic language allows for a deeper level of communication, bypassing the bounds of the rational mind and inviting individuals to explore and contemplate the mysteries of existence.

The use of symbolism in *theurgy*-breathed literature and drama allows for multiple layers of meaning and interpretation. It encourages readers and audiences to engage actively with the text or performance, decoding the symbolic elements and discovering their personal importance and resonance. Symbolism creates a bridge between the mundane and the transcendent, inviting individuals to explore the deeper dimensions of reality.

The narrative structure of *theurgy*-breathed literature and drama often mirrors the quest of the soul towards union with the divine. The protagonist's quest, challenges, and transformation reflect the spiritual quest of the individual seeking to awaken their inherent divine nature.

These narratives often explore themes like the soul's longing for reunion with the divine, the *purification* of the soul, the cultivation of virtues, and the transformative power of love and devotion. The characters and their experiences provide archetypal representations of the spiritual path, inviting readers and audiences to reflect upon their own quest and contemplate the possibilities of spiritual growth and transformation.

Theurgy-breathed literature and drama also often depict encounters with *divine beings,* celestial realms, and supernatural phenomena. These encounters serve as catalysts for spiritual awakening and the integration of the divine into the human experience. They convey the sense of wonder, awe, and *transcendence* that can arise from *theurgy*-breathed practices and experiences.

The use of dramatic elements in *theurgy*-breathed literature and drama enhances the emotional effect and immersive quality of the *work.* The portrayal of conflicts, dilemmas, and moments of revelation creates a dynamic and engaging narrative that vibes with readers and audiences.

The dramatic representation of *theurgy*-breathed themes allows for a visceral and experiential engagement with the transformative power of *theurgy*. It enables individuals to witness and emotionally connect with the processes of spiritual awakening, *purification*, and union with the divine. Drama provides a platform for the portrayal of intense emotions, catharsis, and the *transcendence* of ordinary reality.

Theurgy-breathed literature and drama also explore the relationship between the individual and the divine, as well as the enmeshment of all beings and the *divine source*. These works often depict the effect of the *divine presence* on human lives, the place of divine intervention or guidance, and the consequences of aligning with or deviating from the *divine will*.

The characters in *theurgy*-breathed literature and drama often serve as archetypes, embodying different aspects of the human experience and the spiritual quest. Through their struggles, triumphs, and transformations, readers and audiences can identify with these characters, realize their own potential for growth and spiritual realization, and find inspiration for their own path.

The portrayal of rituals, ceremonies, and *theur-gical practices* is another significant aspect of *theurgy*-breathed literature and drama. These works often incorporate scenes or descriptions of spiritual practices, invocations, and symbolic gestures that evoke the transformative power of *theurgy*.

The representation of rituals and practices in literature and drama allows individuals to witness and vicariously participate in the transformative processes of *theurgy*. It provides insights into the inner workings of spiritual practices and the potential for personal and collective transformation.

Theurgy-breathed literature and drama can be a source of inspiration, guidance, and reflection for individuals on their spiritual quest. They invite readers and audiences to explore the depths of their own being, contemplate the mysteries of existence, and engage with the transformative power of the divine.

In culmination, *theurgy* and *theurgy*-breathed literature and drama are interconnected expressions of mystical and spiritual traditions. These literary and dramatic works convey the transformative power of *theurgy* through symbolism, narrative, and dramatic elements. They explore themes like the soul's longing for reunion with the divine, the *purification* of the soul, and the transformative power of love and devotion. The use of symbolism allows for deeper levels of meaning and interpretation, while the narrative structure and dramatic elements enhance the emotional effect and immersive quality of the works. The portrayal of rituals and practices provides insights into the transformative processes of *theurgy* and invites individuals to contemplate their own spiritual quest. *Theurgy*-breathed literature and drama can serve as a source of inspiration, guidance, and reflection, inviting individuals to engage with the transformative power of the divine and explore the mysteries of existence.

XVIII: Divine Names and Attributes

Theurgy and the concept of *divine names and attributes* are intricately connected within mystical and spiritual traditions. In Greek, the term for divine names is "θεία ονόματα" (theía onómata) and the term for attributes is "ιδιότητες" (idiótites).

Divine names and attributes refer to the various names, titles, and qualities attributed to the divine in religious and mystical traditions. They are used to describe and invoke different aspects of the divine nature, serving as a means to connect with and understand the *divine presence*.

In the context of *theurgy*, the use of *divine names and attributes* is a central practice for invoking and establishing a connection with the *divine realms*. *Theurgy* recognizes that the divine is multifaceted, and the use of different names and attributes helps to express and access different aspects of the divine reality.

The *divine names and attributes* are often regarded as sacred and powerful, representing the *divine qualities*, energies, and manifestations. They are seen as portals or gateways that open pathways for communication, communion, and union with the divine.

The *invocation* of *divine names and attributes* in *theurgy* serves a few purposes. Firstly, it acts as a means of reverence and devotion, acknowledging the *divine presence* and expressing a deep respect for the divine nature. Through the use of sacred names and attributes, individuals realize and honor the *divine qualities* and express their longing for connection and union.

Secondly, the *invocation* of *divine names and attributes* is a way of attuning oneself to specific *divine energies* or qualities. Each divine name and attribute stands for a particular aspect of the divine nature, like love, wisdom, compassion, or power. By invoking these names and attributes, individuals seek to align themselves with the corresponding *divine qualities*, allowing these qualities to manifest within themselves.

The use of *divine names and attributes* can also serve as a means of *contemplation* and *meditation*. By sharpening on a particular name or attribute, individuals dive into to submarina of its meaning and seek to understand its importance in relation to the divine nature. This *contemplation* can lead to insights, revelations, and a deeper understanding of the divine mysteries.

In addition to their devotional and contemplative functions, *divine names and attributes* are used in *theurgy* for the purpose of invoking *divine presence*, receiving guidance, and participating in the transformative power of the divine. Through the recitation or *meditation* on specific divine names, individuals seek to establish a direct connection with the *divine realms* and experience the transformative influence of the *divine energies*.

Divine names and attributes can also serve as a means of protection, healing, and spiritual empowerment. In *theurgy*, certain names or combinations of names are believed to possess specific qualities that can provide spiritual guidance, aid in overcoming obstacles, or facilitate healing on various levels.

The concept of *divine names and attributes* is not limited to a single tradition but is present in various mystical and religious traditions worldwide. For example, in the Kabbalistic tradition of Judaism, the use of the *divine names and attributes* is a central practice for attaining spiritual insight and union with the divine. Each Hebrew letter and its corresponding divine name is determined to hold revelatory mystical importance.

In Islamic mysticism, known as Sufism, the *invocation* of the divine names (the "asma al-husna") is a central practice. The 99 names of Allah represent the various qualities and attributes of the divine, and their recitation is believed to lead to spiritual *purification*, enlightenment, and the realization of the *divine presence*.

In Hinduism, the recitation of mantras, which consist of divine names or sacred syllables, is a common practice in the pursuit of spiritual awakening and communion with the divine. Each mantra is believed to represent a specific aspect of the divine and has transformative effects when chanted with devotion and intention.

In the Neoplatonic tradition, *divine names and attributes* play an important place in *theurgy*. They are used to invoke and align with specific aspects of the *divine hierarchy* and participate in the *divine energies* and intentions. The *invocation* of *divine names and attributes* is seen as a means of ascending through the levels of reality, purifying the soul, and attaining union with the divine.

In culmination, *theurgy* and the concept of *divine names and attributes* are intimately connected within mystical and spiritual traditions. The *invocation* of *divine names and attributes* acts as a means of connecting with and understanding the divine nature, expressing reverence and devotion, attuning oneself to specific *divine energies*, and participating in the transformative power of the divine. *Divine names and attributes* are regarded as sacred and powerful, representing different aspects of the divine reality. Their use in *theurgy* allows individuals to establish a direct connection with the *divine realms*, seek spiritual guidance, and experience the transformative influence of the *divine energies*. The concept of *divine names and attributes* is present in various mystical and religious traditions worldwide and is employed as a means of spiritual *purification*, enlightenment, and the realization of the *divine presence*.

XIX: THEURGY AND MAGIC

The relationship between *theurgy* and magic is a complex and often debated topic within mystical and esoteric traditions. In Greek, the term for magic is "μαγεία" (mageía), and the term for *theurgy* is "θεουργία" (theourgía).

Theurgy and magic share certain similarities, but they also have distinct characteristics and purposes. Understanding their relationship requires exploring their underlying principles, goals, and methods.

Magic, in its broadest sense, refers to practices that seek to influence or manipulate natural or supernatural forces to achieve desired outcomes. It involves the use of rituals, spells, *talismans*, and various techniques to tap into hidden powers or unseen realms. The purpose of magic can range from practical matters, like healing, protection, and *divination*, to more ambitious goals, like gaining power, wealth, or control.

Theurgy, on the other hand, is a spiritual practice that aims to establish a direct and conscious connection with the divine. It involves engaging in rituals, contemplative practices, and spiritual disciplines to align oneself with the *divine will*, awaken the latent divine nature within, and achieve union with the divine. *Theurgy* is focused on the transformation of the individual, the cultivation of virtues, and the realization of the *divine presence*.

While both *theurgy* and magic involve ritualistic practices and the use of symbolism, their underlying intentions and orientations differ significantly. Magic is often associated with personal desires, egoic ambitions, and the manipulation of external circumstances for individual gain. It can involve the use of incantations, invocations, and the manipulation of energies to manifest specific outcomes.

Theurgy, on the other hand, is ineradicable from a deeper spiritual quest for union with the divine and the realization of one's inherent divinity. It is concerned with transcending the ego and aligning oneself with divine principles, qualities, and energies. *Theurgy* seeks to encourage virtues, purify the soul, and participate in the divine creative process.

The distinction between *theurgy* and magic is often seen in their respective ethical frameworks. *Theurgy* tends to emphasize the importance of ethical conduct, selflessness, and the alignment of one's will with the *divine will*. The ethical dimension is determined important in the spiritual transformation and the attainment of union with the divine.

Magic, on the other hand, does not necessarily adhere to a specific ethical code. While some magical traditions promote ethical principles and caution against harmful practices, magic itself is often seen as morally neutral. The ethical implications of magic largely depend on the intentions and actions of the practitioner.

It is important to note that the line between *theurgy* and magic can be blurry at times, and there can be overlap and influence between the two. *Theurgy*-breathed practices may incorporate certain magical techniques or symbolism, especially when they serve as a means of accessing and working with subtle energies or realms.

Likewise, magical traditions can incorporate elements of *theurgy* when they realize and seek to establish a connection with higher powers or spiritual dimensions. In some cases, the line between *theurgy* and magic may be a matter of perspective and interpretation, as different mystical traditions may emphasize different aspects or approaches.

One of the key differences between *theurgy* and magic is the source of power and authority. In *theurgy*, the power is believed to come from the *divine source* itself. The theurgist seeks to align with the *divine will* and participate in the divine creative process. *Theurgical practices* involve invoking divine names, engaging in rituals, and cultivating virtues to establish a conscious connection with the divine.

In magic, the power is often believed to be derived from the manipulation of natural or supernatural forces. Magical practices may involve invoking spirits, working with *symbols*, and performing rituals to tap into hidden powers or influence the course of events. The focus is on the practitioner's ability to manipulate and harness these forces for desired outcomes.

Another distinction between *theurgy* and magic lies in their ultimate aims. *Theurgy* seeks union with the divine and the realization of one's divine nature. It is driven by a deep longing for spiritual growth, enlightenment, and the transformation of consciousness. *Theurgical practices* are aimed at transcending the bounds of the ego and participating in the divine creative process.

Magic, on the other hand, is often driven by more immediate and tangible goals. It may aim to manifest specific outcomes, gain power, protection, or fulfill personal desires. The focus is on the practical and worldly aspects of life, rather than on the spiritual evolution or union with the divine.

The relationship between *theurgy* and magic can vary depending on the specific mystical or esoteric tradition. Some traditions view the two as incompatible, with *theurgy* representing a higher, more spiritual path, while magic is seen as a lower, more mundane endeavor. In these traditions, *theurgy* is determined a means of *transcendence* and union with the divine, while magic is perceived as a more limited and ego-centered pursuit.

However, other traditions view *theurgy* and magic as complementary practices that can be integrated within a broader spiritual scaffolding. They realize that both *theurgy* and magic can serve as means of accessing hidden dimensions of reality and cultivating a deeper connection with the divine. These traditions may emphasize the ethical dimension, the intention behind the practices, and the cultivation of virtues to ensure that the magical practices remain aligned with the spiritual path.

In culmination, the relationship between *theurgy* and magic is complex and multifaceted. While they share some similarities in terms of ritualistic practices and the use of symbolism, the underlying intentions, orientations, and ethical frameworks of *theurgy* and magic differ significantly. *Theurgy* is focused on the spiritual transformation, the realization of one's inherent divinity, and the attainment of union with the divine. Magic, on the other hand, often wants to influence or manipulate natural or supernatural forces to achieve desired outcomes. The distinction between *theurgy* and magic lies in their underlying intentions, sources of power, ethical frameworks, and ultimate goals. While there can be overlap and influence between the two, the precise relationship between *theurgy* and magic depends on the specific mystical or esoteric tradition and its interpretation of these practices.

XX: ETHICS AND MORAL PHILOSOPHY

Theurgy and *theurgy*-breathed ethics and moral philosophy are intimately connected within mystical and spiritual traditions. In Greek, the term for ethics is "ηθική" (ēthikē), and the term for moral philosophy is "ηθική φιλοσοφία" (ēthikē philosophía).

Theurgy-breathed ethics and moral philosophy provide a scaffolding for understanding and guiding human behavior in alignment with divine principles and intentions. They emphasize the cultivation of virtues, the pursuit of ethical conduct, and the realization of one's inherent divinity.

One of the central principles of *theurgy*-breathed ethics is the recognition of the divine as the ultimate source of morality and the highest standard of conduct. It acknowledges that the divine embodies perfect qualities and virtues and that human beings are called to emulate and embody these qualities in their thoughts, actions, and relationships.

Theurgy-breathed ethics highlights the cultivation of virtues as a means to align oneself with the divine. Virtues are determined inherent qualities of the divine nature and include qualities like love, compassion, wisdom, courage, justice, and humility. The cultivation of virtues is seen as a transformative process that leads to personal growth, spiritual realization, and alignment with the *divine will*.

Theurgy-breathed ethics recognizes the enmeshment of all beings and the moral responsibility that arises from this enmeshment. It highlights the importance of recognizing the *divine presence* in oneself and others and treating all beings with respect, compassion, and fairness. The ethical scaffolding extends beyond human beings and includes the natural world, acknowledging the enmeshment and interdependence of all aspects of creation.

The concept of moral responsibility in *theurgy*-breathed ethics extends beyond the world of individual actions and includes the intention behind those actions. It highlights the importance of aligning one's intentions with *divine will* and acting in accordance with the highest ethical principles. The focus is not solely on external behavior but also on cultivating a virtuous character and an ethical mindset.

Theurgy-breathed ethics places a strong emphasis on self-reflection, self-examination, and self-transformation. It encourages individuals to engage in practices like *meditation, contemplation,* and introspection to develop self-awareness, identify and address personal shortcomings, and encourage virtues.

Theurgy-breathed ethics recognizes the transformative power of ethical conduct and the cultivation of virtues. It acknowledges that ethical behavior not just contributes to personal growth and spiritual realization but also has a ripple effect on the collective consciousness and the harmonious unfolding of creation. The ethical choices and actions of individuals can effect the wellness of others and contribute to the overall spiritual evolution of humanity.

Theurgy-breathed ethics also recognizes the importance of intention and motivation in ethical conduct. It highlights that ethical actions should be guided by selflessness, compassion, and a genuine desire to serve the highest good. The intention behind an *action* is determined important, as it reflects the state of consciousness and the alignment with the divine principles.

Theurgy-breathed ethics encourages individuals to seek harmony and balance in all aspects of life. It recognizes that the pursuit of material wealth, power, or personal gain should not overshadow the higher spiritual values and the cultivation of virtues. The ethical scaffolding highlights the need for discernment, moderation, and the recognition of the transient nature of material possessions.

The concept of *divine love* is central to *theurgy*-breathed ethics. *Divine love* is seen as a transformative force that goes beyond personal attachments and preferences. *Theurgy*-breathed ethics encourages individuals to encourage a sense of universal love and compassion, extending care and support to all beings. It recognizes that love and compassion are essential qualities for spiritual growth, the realization of one's inherent divinity, and the encouraging of harmonious relationships within the interconnected nexus of existence.

Theurgy-breathed ethics also highlights the importance of forgiveness, reconciliation, and the resolution of conflicts. It recognizes that human beings are prone to making mistakes and experiencing conflicts, but it promotes the idea that these challenges can serve as opportunities for growth, healing, and spiritual development. The ethical scaffolding encourages individuals to seek resolution through dialogue, understanding, and forgiveness, promoting harmony and unity among individuals and communities.

The practice of *theurgy* itself is deeply ineradicable from ethical principles. *Theurgy* involves engaging in rituals, invocations, and spiritual disciplines with the intention of aligning oneself with the *divine will* and participating in the divine creative process. *Theurgy*-breathed ethics provides guidelines for ethical conduct during these practices, emphasizing the importance of sincerity, reverence, and respect for the *divine presence*.

In culmination, *theurgy* and *theurgy*-breathed ethics and moral philosophy are inseparable within mystical and spiritual traditions. *Theurgy*-breathed ethics provides a scaffolding for guiding human behavior in alignment with divine principles and intentions. It highlights the cultivation of virtues, the pursuit of ethical conduct, and the realization of one's inherent divinity. The ethical scaffolding recognizes the divine as the ultimate source of morality and highlights the importance of emulating *divine qualities* and virtues. *Theurgy*-breathed ethics acknowledges the enmeshment of all beings and the moral responsibility that arises from this enmeshment. It recognizes the transformative power of ethical conduct and the cultivation of virtues for personal growth, spiritual realization, and the harmonious unfolding of creation. The ethical scaffolding highlights self-reflection, self-transformation, and the cultivation of a virtuous character. It promotes universal love, compassion, forgiveness, and the resolution of conflicts. The practice of *theurgy* itself is ineradicable from ethical principles, emphasizing sincerity, reverence, and respect for the *divine presence*. *Theurgy*-breathed ethics provides guidance for ethical conduct during *theurgy* practices and supports the alignment with the *divine will*.

μαντεία

προφητεία

XXI: Divine Revelation

Theurgy and the concept of divine revelation are closely intertwined within mystical and spiritual traditions. In Greek, the term for divine revelation is "θεία αποκάλυψη" (theía apokálypsi), and the term for *theurgy* is "θεουργία" (theourgía).

Divine revelation refers to the communication of divine truths, insights, and knowledge to human beings. It is the manifestation of *divine wisdom*, guidance, and understanding in a way that goes beyond ordinary human perception and intellect.

The concept of divine revelation recognizes that there are aspects of reality, truth, and the divine nature that exceed the limits of human comprehension. It acknowledges that the divine can reveal itself to individuals through various means, like direct experiences, visions, dreams, breathed writings, or spiritual insights.

In the context of *theurgy*, divine revelation holds a central place in the quest for spiritual growth, understanding, and union with the divine. *Theurgy* seeks to establish a conscious and direct connection with the *divine realms*, allowing individuals to receive and assimilate *divine knowledge*, insights, and guidance.

Divine revelation in *theurgy* is not limited to intellectual understanding or the acquisition of information. It involves a deeper level of insight and knowing that goes beyond the rational mind. It includes the direct experience and realization of the *divine presence*, the understanding of spiritual truths, and the transformation of consciousness.

Theurgy recognizes that divine revelation can occur through various channels and modalities. It can happen in moments of revelatory spiritual experiences, where individuals have direct encounters with the divine or go beyond ordinary states of consciousness. These experiences can be accompanied by feelings of awe, wonder, and a sense of being in the presence of something greater than oneself.

Divine revelation can also occur through the practice of contemplative and meditative techniques. By quieting the mind, opening the heart, and sharpening one's attention inward, individuals create a receptive space for divine insights and inspirations to arise. In these states of deep inner stillness, individuals may receive revelations, intuitions, or spiritual guidance that illuminates their understanding and path.

The use of rituals and spiritual practices in *theurgy* can also facilitate divine revelation. Through the *invocation* of divine names, the recitation of prayers, the performance of sacred ceremonies, and the engagement in symbolic gestures, individuals create a sacred space that invites *divine presence* and revelation. These rituals serve as a means of opening oneself to the divine influx and establishing a direct line of communication with the *divine realms.*

Divine revelation in *theurgy* is not seen as a one-sided process but as a co-creative interaction between the divine and the individual. It involves active participation and receptivity on the part of the individual, as well as divine grace and guidance. The individual seeks to attune oneself to the *divine will*, encourage virtues, and purify the soul, creating conditions conducive to receiving divine revelations.

The concept of divine revelation in *theurgy* is often associated with the idea of divine grace. Divine grace is the unmerited favor and assistance bestowed upon individuals by the divine. It is believed that through sincere devotion, spiritual practice, and the cultivation of virtues, individuals can open themselves to the flow of divine grace, which can lead to revelatory spiritual experiences and revelations.

Divine revelation in *theurgy* can have a transformative effect on individuals. It can bring about shifts in consciousness, deepening of spiritual understanding, and a sense of alignment with the divine purpose. It can provide insights into reality, the purpose of existence, and the enmeshment of all beings.

Theurgy recognizes that divine revelation is not limited to a select few or to specific historical periods. It acknowledges that individuals from all walks of life and across different cultures and traditions can receive divine revelations. The form and content of divine revelations may vary depending on the cultural and individual context, but the underlying truth and transformative power remain universal.

Divine revelation in *theurgy* is often accompanied by a sense of responsibility and a call to *action*. Individuals who receive divine revelations are often called to embody and manifest the *divine qualities* and principles in their lives. They are encouraged to share their insights, teachings, and revelations with others, encouraging spiritual growth and collective awakening.

It is important to note that divine revelation in *theurgy* is not without its challenges and potential pitfalls. The recognition and interpretation of divine revelations require discernment, humility, and a deep understanding of the ethical and moral dimensions of the spiritual path. Individuals need to encourage a healthy balance between personal experiences and the guidance of tradition, community, and ethical principles.

In culmination, *theurgy* and the concept of divine revelation are intertwined within mystical and spiritual traditions. Divine revelation refers to the communication of divine truths, insights, and knowledge to human beings. It recognizes that there are aspects of reality and the divine nature that exceed the limits of human comprehension. Divine revelation holds a central place in *theurgy*, as it allows individuals to receive and assimilate *divine knowledge*, insights, and guidance. It can occur through direct spiritual experiences, contemplative practices, rituals, and the cultivation of virtues. Divine revelation involves a deeper level of insight and knowing that goes beyond the rational mind and leads to the transformation of consciousness. It is a co-creative process between the divine and the individual, often accompanied by a sense of responsibility and a call to embody and manifest the *divine qualities*. Divine revelation in *theurgy* requires discernment, humility, and an understanding of the ethical and moral dimensions of the spiritual path. It is a universal phenomenon that can occur in different cultural and individual contexts, encouraging spiritual growth and collective awakening.

XXII: ALTERED STATES OF CONSCIOUSNESS

Theurgical techniques for achieving altered states of consciousness are an integral part of mystical and spiritual traditions. These techniques, often referred to as "μεταβαλλόντα καταστάσεις συνείδησης" (metavallónta katastáseis synídisis) in Greek, involve various practices that induce shifts in perception, awareness, and experience, allowing individuals to access deeper levels of consciousness and spiritual insight.

Altered states of consciousness are characterized by a departure from ordinary waking consciousness, enabling individuals to go beyond the bounds of the ego and access realms of heightened perception, intuition, and spiritual awareness. These states can range from subtle shifts in awareness to revelatory mystical experiences of unity, *transcendence*, and expanded perception.

Theurgy-breathed techniques for achieving altered states of consciousness include a wide range of practices, each with its unique approach and purpose. Some of these techniques include *meditation*, breathwork, chanting, visualization, sensory deprivation, rhythmic movement, and the use of sacred substances or sacraments.

Meditation is one of the most common and widely practiced techniques for achieving altered states of consciousness. It involves sharpening the mind, calming the mental chatter, and entering a state of deep relaxation and heightened awareness. By cultivating single-pointed concentration, individuals can go beyond ordinary thoughts and perceptions, accessing deeper levels of consciousness and spiritual insight.

Breathwork is another powerful technique used in *theurgy* to induce altered states of consciousness. Through specific breathing patterns and techniques, individuals can regulate the flow of necessary energy (prana or pneuma) in the body, facilitating a shift in consciousness and opening doors to transcendent experiences.

Chanting, the repetition of sacred sounds or mantras, is employed in *theurgy* to alter consciousness. The rhythmic and melodic patterns of chanting have a revelatory effect on the mind and body, inducing a state of focused awareness, deep relaxation, and heightened receptivity to the divine.

Visualization is a technique used in *theurgy* to create mental imagery and harness the power of the mind to induce altered states of consciousness. By imagining specific *symbols*, scenes, or *divine qualities*, individuals can enter into a heightened state of awareness and connect with the subtle realms of existence.

Sensory deprivation is a technique that involves limiting external sensory input to induce altered states of consciousness. This can be achieved through practices like being in a dark and quiet environment or using blindfolds and earplugs. By reducing sensory stimulation, individuals can direct their attention inward and experience heightened states of awareness and perception.

Rhythmic movement, like dancing, drumming, or repetitive physical exercises, is employed in *theurgy* to induce altered states of consciousness. The rhythmic patterns and movements synchronize the body and mind, leading to a state of trance-like absorption, expanded awareness, and connection with the divine.

The use of sacred substances or sacraments, like certain herbs, plants, or entheogens, is present in some mystical traditions as a means of achieving altered states of consciousness. These substances are believed to have the potential to open the doors of perception and facilitate transcendent experiences. It is important to note that the use of sacred substances should be approached with caution, respect, and in accordance with ethical guidelines and legal regulations.

The specific techniques employed in *theurgy* to achieve altered states of consciousness can vary across different mystical traditions and practices. The choice of technique often depends on the individual's inclination, cultural context, and the goals of the spiritual quest. *Theurgy*-breathed techniques aim to facilitate a temporary departure from ordinary waking consciousness, enabling individuals to access deeper layers of awareness, spiritual insight, and connection with the divine.

Achieving altered states of consciousness through *theurgy* is not an end in itself but a means to deepen the spiritual experience and facilitate personal transformation. These states provide an opportunity to go beyond the bounds of the ego, expand one's perception of reality, and gain insights into the nature of existence and the divine.

It is important to note that *theurgy* places a strong emphasis on ethical conduct, self-discipline, and a balanced approach to the use of altered states of consciousness. The ethical dimension acts as a guiding principle to ensure that the pursuit of altered states aligns with the highest spiritual ideals and is integrated into a holistic and responsible spiritual path.

Furthermore, the use of altered states of consciousness in *theurgy* is often accompanied by specific intentions and purposes. These may include seeking spiritual guidance, engaging in *divine communion*, cultivating virtues, purifying the soul, and participating in the divine creative process. The focus is on using these altered states as tools for self-discovery, spiritual growth, and the realization of one's inherent divinity.

In culmination, *theurgy* employs various techniques for achieving altered states of consciousness, enabling individuals to go beyond ordinary waking consciousness and access deeper levels of awareness and spiritual insight. These techniques include *meditation*, breathwork, chanting, visualization, sensory deprivation, rhythmic movement, and the use of sacred substances or sacraments. Altered states of consciousness in *theurgy* serve as a means to deepen the spiritual experience, gain insights into the nature of existence, and establish a connection with the divine. The use of these techniques is guided by ethical principles, responsible practices, and specific intentions aligned with spiritual growth and transformation. *Theurgy*-breathed techniques for achieving altered states of consciousness provide valuable tools for individuals on the spiritual path, facilitating self-discovery, personal transformation, and the realization of one's inherent divinity.

θεουργικές πρακτικές

XXIII: THEORIES OF KNOWLEDGE AND EPISTEMOLOGY

Theurgy and *theurgy*-breathed theories of knowledge and epistemology dive into the nature of knowledge, the sources of knowledge, and the ways in which individuals can attain deeper understanding and insight. In Greek, the term for knowledge is "γνώση" (gnósi), and the term for epistemology is "επιστημολογία" (epistemología).

Theurgy recognizes that there are different forms of knowledge and that not all knowledge can be acquired through ordinary means. It acknowledges that there are dimensions of reality and aspects of the divine that go beyond rational understanding and require direct experiential knowledge.

Theurgy-breathed theories of knowledge emphasize the importance of direct spiritual experience as a means of acquiring knowledge. It posits that true knowledge is not merely intellectual or theoretical but is based on personal experience and the direct apprehension of spiritual truths.

One of the central tenets of *theurgy*-breathed epistemology is the concept of "gnosis." Gnosis refers to a direct, intuitive, and experiential knowledge that goes beyond the bounds of ordinary perception and intellect. It is a form of knowledge that arises from a deep inner realization, often accompanied by a sense of unity, enmeshment, and spiritual insight.

Theurgy-breathed theories of knowledge realize that gnosis can be attained through various means, including mystical experiences, contemplative practices, the cultivation of virtues, and the engagement in theurgical rituals. These practices aim to quiet the mind, open the heart, and create conditions conducive to the direct experience of spiritual truths.

Mystical experiences play a significant place in *theurgy*-breathed epistemology. These experiences involve a temporary suspension of ordinary consciousness and the direct apprehension of divine realities. Mystical experiences can range from subtle moments of *transcendence* to revelatory states of unity, ecstasy, and illumination.

Contemplative practices, like *meditation*, are also fundamental to *theurgy*-breathed epistemology. By quieting the mind and cultivating single-pointed focus, individuals create a receptive space for spiritual insights and direct knowledge to emerge. Through the practice of sustained attention and inner stillness, individuals can go beyond ordinary mental processes and access deeper levels of understanding and realization.

The cultivation of virtues is another aspect of *theurgy*-breathed epistemology. *Theurgy* recognizes that the development of virtuous qualities, like love, compassion, wisdom, and humility, enhances one's receptivity to spiritual truths and deepens one's capacity for direct knowledge. Virtues are seen as transformative qualities that align individuals with the divine and open doors to spiritual insight.

Engaging in theurgical rituals and practices is determined a means of acquiring knowledge in *theurgy*-breathed epistemology. These rituals involve the *invocation* of divine names, the performance of symbolic gestures, and the cultivation of a reverent and receptive mindset. By actively participating in these rituals, individuals create a sacred space for the direct experience of *divine presence* and the reception of spiritual insights.

Theurgy-breathed theories of knowledge also acknowledge the bounds of rational and intellectual understanding. While rational thinking and logical analysis have their place in acquiring knowledge, they are seen as insufficient for apprehending the deeper truths of the spiritual world. *Theurgy* recognizes that direct experience, intuition, and the cultivation of inner wisdom are essential for gaining a more comprehensive understanding of reality.

The concept of revelation is central to *theurgy*-breathed epistemology. Divine revelation refers to the communication of spiritual truths, insights, and knowledge from the divine to human beings. It is seen as a means of acquiring knowledge that surpasses ordinary human understanding and is based on direct communication with the divine.

Divine revelation can occur through various channels, like mystical experiences, breathed writings, visions, dreams, or intuitive insights. *Theurgy*-breathed epistemology recognizes the importance of being receptive to divine revelations and actively seeking spiritual guidance to deepen one's knowledge and understanding.

Theurgy-breathed theories of knowledge also emphasize the place of personal transformation and *purification* in acquiring deeper insights and understanding. The cultivation of virtues, the *purification* of the soul, and the alignment with divine principles are seen as essential prerequisites for attaining higher knowledge. As individuals undergo inner *purification* and spiritual growth, they become more attuned to spiritual truths and gain access to higher levels of knowledge.

Theurgy-breathed epistemology recognizes that knowledge is not solely an individual pursuit but is also shaped by social and cultural factors. It acknowledges that different mystical traditions and spiritual paths may have unique perspectives on knowledge and epistemology. The concept of a spiritual community or lineage, where knowledge is transmitted from teacher to student, is often seen as significant in *theurgy*-breathed theories of knowledge.

In culmination, *theurgy* and *theurgy*-breathed theories of knowledge and epistemology focus on the nature of knowledge, the sources of knowledge, and the ways in which individuals can attain deeper under-standing and insight. *Theurgy*-breathed epistemology highlights the importance of direct spiritual experience, personal transformation, and the cultivation of virtues in acquiring knowledge. It recognizes the bounds of rational and intellectual understanding and highlights the place of mystical experiences, contemplative prac-tices, and the engagement in theurgical rituals in access-ing higher knowledge. *Theurgy*-breathed epistemology acknowledges the concept of gnosis, a direct and intu-itive knowledge that goes beyond ordinary perception and intellect. It also recognizes the place of revelation in acquiring spiritual truths and understanding. The concept of revelation highlights the importance of be-ing receptive to divine guidance and actively seeking spiritual insight. *Theurgy*-breathed theories of knowledge realize the social and cultural dimensions of knowledge and often emphasize the place of spiritual communities or lineages in the transmission of knowledge. Overall, *theurgy*-breathed theories of knowledge and epistemology provide a scaffolding for understanding and pursuing deeper levels of understanding, insight, and spiritual realization.

XXIV: THEURGY-BREATHED COMMUNITY AND SOCIAL ORGANIZATION

Theurgy and the concept of *theurgy*-breathed community and social organization are interconnected aspects within mystical and spiritual traditions. In Greek, the term for community is "κοινότητα" (koinótita), and the term for social organization is "κοινωνική οργάνωση" (koinonikí organósi).

Theurgy-breathed community refers to a group of individuals who share a common spiritual path, values, and goals. It is a community that is united by a shared commitment to the pursuit of spiritual growth, the realization of *divine qualities*, and the engagement in *theurgical practices*.

Theurgy-breathed communities often provide a supportive and nurturing environment for individuals on the spiritual path. They offer opportunities for mutual learning, inspiration, and the exchange of spiritual insights and experiences. These communities encourage a sense of belonging, camaraderie, and shared purpose, creating a space for individuals to deepen their spiritual practice and integrate spiritual principles into their daily lives.

The concept of community in *theurgy*-breathed traditions goes beyond mere social interaction. It highlights the importance of spiritual companionship and the recognition of the *divine presence* in one another. *Theurgy*-breathed communities strive to create an atmosphere of love, compassion, and mutual respect, where individuals can find support, guidance, and inspiration on their spiritual quest.

Theurgy-breathed communities often have a spiritual leader or teacher who acts as a guide and mentor. The place of the spiritual leader is to provide guidance, instruction, and support to individuals on the spiritual path. They embody the principles and teachings of the tradition, serving as a living example of the transformative power of *theurgy* and spiritual practice.

The concept of social organization in *theurgy*-breathed traditions refers to the ways in which these communities are structured and function. Social organization includes various aspects, like leadership roles, decision-making processes, shared responsibilities, and the establishment of communal practices and rituals.

In some *theurgy*-breathed traditions, the social organization is hierarchical, with a clear structure of authority and roles. There may be different levels of initiation or spiritual attainment, and individuals progress through these levels as they deepen their understanding and experience of *theurgy*. The hierarchical structure ensures a smooth transmission of teachings and practices, as well as the preservation of the tradition's integrity and authenticity.

Other *theurgy*-breathed communities may adopt a more egalitarian or decentralized social organization. These communities emphasize the importance of individual autonomy, personal responsibility, and the cultivation of inner wisdom. Decision-making processes may involve collective discussion, consensus-building, or shared leadership, allowing each individual to contribute their unique insights and perspectives.

Theurgy-breathed communities often have shared rituals and practices that help encourage a sense of unity and connection among members. These rituals can include the *invocation* of divine names, the recitation of prayers or mantras, the performance of sacred ceremonies, and communal acts of service. The shared practices create a collective energy and a sacred atmosphere that support individual and collective spiritual growth.

Theurgy-breathed communities also realize the importance of service and the practice of virtues in social interactions. The cultivation of virtues like love, compassion, humility, and generosity is determined essential for harmonious relationships and the wellness of the community as a whole. Members of the community are encouraged to support and uplift one another, to be of service to those in need, and to contribute to the greater good.

The concept of community in *theurgy*-breathed traditions extends beyond the bounds of the immediate community itself. These communities often engage in outreach activities, charitable *work*, or educational initiatives to share their spiritual insights and practices with the wider society. They strive to embody and promote values of peace, compassion, and spiritual awakening, contributing to the positive transformation of the world.

Theurgy-breathed communities realize the enmeshment of all beings and the interdependence of the individual and the collective. They acknowledge that spiritual growth and transformation are not isolated pursuits but are intricately linked to the wellness and evolution of the larger social fabric. The spiritual practices and teachings of theurgy are seen as catalysts for personal and collective awakening, encouraging a sense of responsibility and engagement with the world.

In culmination, theurgy and the concept of theurgy-breathed community and social organization emphasize the importance of supportive and nurturing environments for individuals on the spiritual path. Theurgy-breathed communities provide a space for individuals to deepen their spiritual practice, exchange insights, and receive support and guidance from spiritual leaders or mentors. These communities encourage a sense of belonging and shared purpose, creating an atmosphere of love, compassion, and mutual respect. The

social organization of *theurgy*-breathed communities
may vary, ranging from hierarchical structures to more
egalitarian or decentralized models. Shared rituals and
practices help encourage a sense of unity and connection among members. The cultivation of virtues and the
practice of service are seen as integral to harmonious
relationships and the wellness of the community. The
concept of community in *theurgy*-breathed traditions
extends beyond the immediate community, encompassing outreach activities and a commitment to contribute
to the greater good of society. *Theurgy*-breathed communities realize the enmeshment of all beings and the
place of spiritual practice in personal and collective
awakening. These communities embody and promote
values of peace, compassion, and spiritual awakening,
contributing to the positive transformation of the
world.

XXV: Neoplatonic Mysticism

Theurgy holds a central place in Neoplatonic mysticism, an ancient philosophical and spiritual tradition that emerged during the Hellenistic period and flourished during Late Antiquity. In Greek, the term for *theurgy* is "θεουργία" (theourgía), which means "divine *work*" or "divine *action*."

Neoplatonic mysticism, heavily influenced by the teachings of the philosopher Plotinus, seeks to attain union with the divine through a process of spiritual ascent and transformation. It recognizes the ultimate reality as a transcendent and ineffable One, which emanates a hierarchical order of beings, culminating in the divine intellect and the divine soul.

Theurgy, within Neoplatonic mysticism, is a set of spiritual practices and rituals aimed at establishing a direct connection with the *divine realms* and facilitating the union of the soul with the divine. It is seen as a means of participation in the divine *work* and the alignment of the soul with the higher realms of existence.

One of the fundamental principles of Neoplatonic mysticism is the concept of "hierarchy" or "the *divine hierarchy*." This concept recognizes the existence of different levels of reality, ranging from the transcendent One to the material world. *Theurgy* acts as a means to traverse these hierarchical levels and to establish a harmonious relationship with the *divine beings* that populate them.

The practice of *theurgy* in Neoplatonic mysticism involves various techniques and rituals, each serving a specific purpose in the process of spiritual ascent. These techniques include *invocation, contemplation, purification*, and the use of *symbols* and rituals.

Invocation is a central aspect of theurgical practice in Neoplatonic mysticism. It involves calling upon and establishing a connection with *divine beings*, like gods, *angels*, or *celestial intelligences*. Through the recitation of sacred names, prayers, or hymns, the practitioner seeks to establish a direct line of communication and communion with these higher beings.

Contemplation is another key practice in Neoplatonic mysticism and *theurgy*. It involves the cultivation of deep inner stillness and the focused *contemplation* of divine forms and principles. Through contemplative practices, the practitioner aims to go beyond the bounds of the material world and to attune their consciousness to the divine realities.

Purification is an essential aspect of theurgical practice in Neoplatonic mysticism. It involves the *purification* of the soul from negative influences, attachments, and impurities that hinder the spiritual ascent. *Purification* can be achieved through ethical conduct, the cultivation of virtues, and the practice of self-discipline. By purifying the soul, the practitioner creates a vessel that is receptive to the divine influx.

Symbols and rituals play a significant place in *theurgy* within Neoplatonic mysticism. *Symbols*, like sacred geometrical shapes, divine names, or hieroglyphs, are used to represent and access the higher realities. Rituals, including the performance of ceremonies, the use of sacraments, or the recitation of prayers, create a sacred space and invoke the presence of the divine. These *symbols* and rituals serve as vehicles for the transmission of *divine energies* and the establishment of a mystical connection.

Theurgy in Neoplatonic mysticism is not merely a means of acquiring knowledge or experiencing *divine presence*; it is a transformative process that targets the union of the soul with the divine. It involves a revelatory reorientation of consciousness and a shift in one's identification from the limited ego to the higher, more expansive divine reality.

The goal of *theurgy* in Neoplatonic mysticism is the mystical union, or "henosis," with the divine. Henosis refers to the merging of the individual soul with the *divine essence*, resulting in a state of ecstatic union and revelatory spiritual realization. It is a transcendent state beyond ordinary human experience, where the bounds of the self dissolve, and the individual becomes one with the divine.

The practice of *theurgy* in Neoplatonic mysticism is not restricted to a select few or to specific religious or cultural contexts. It is determined a universal path, accessible to individuals from different backgrounds and traditions who are sincerely committed to the pursuit of spiritual transformation.

Neoplatonic mysticism and *theurgy* have had a lasting influence on Western esoteric traditions, including Christian mysticism, Kabbalah, and Renaissance occultism. The principles and practices of *theurgy* endure to inspirit seekers and spiritual practitioners, offering a pathway to *transcendence, divine union,* and the realization of one's true nature.

In culmination, *theurgy* holds a central place in Neoplatonic mysticism as a means of establishing a direct connection with the divine and facilitating the union of the soul with the higher realms of existence. It involves various practices like *invocation, contemplation, purification,* and the use of *symbols* and rituals. *Theurgy* is ineradicable from the concept of hierarchy, recognizing the existence of different levels of reality and the *divine hierarchy*. Through the practice of *theurgy*, individuals aim to go beyond the bounds of the material world and to attain mystical union with the divine. *Theurgical practices* in Neoplatonic mysticism have had a revelatory influence on Western esoteric traditions and endure to provide a transformative path for seekers of spiritual realization.

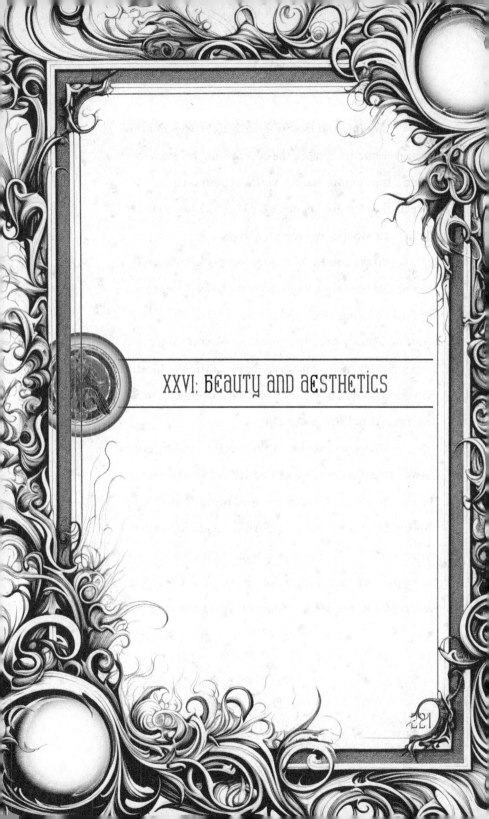

XXVI: Beauty and Aesthetics

Theurgy and *theurgy*-breathed theories of beauty and aesthetics explore the relationship between the divine, the human, and the world of aesthetics. In Greek, the term for beauty is "κάλλος" (kállos), and the term for aesthetics is "αισθητική" (aisthitikí).

In the context of *theurgy*, beauty is not merely a superficial or subjective concept but is deeply intertwined with the divine and the quest for spiritual realization. *Theurgy*-breathed theories of beauty and aesthetics realize that beauty is a manifestation of the divine, a reflection of higher realities, and a means to connect with the transcendent.

Theurgy views beauty as a quality that can evoke a revelatory sense of awe, harmony, and spiritual elevation. It includes not just visual beauty but also the beauty of sound, movement, form, and ideas. *Theurgy*-breathed theories of beauty emphasize the transformative power of beauty in awakening the soul, triggering *contemplation*, and leading individuals closer to the divine.

The concept of beauty in *theurgy* is often associated with the concept of "the Beautiful," or "το Καλόν" (to Kalón) in Greek. The Beautiful stands for the ideal form of beauty, transcending the bounds of the physical world and pointing towards the divine. It is determined a divine principle that radiates harmony, perfection, and spiritual truth.

Theurgy-breathed theories of beauty realize that the experience of beauty is subjective and can vary from individual to individual. However, they also emphasize that genuine beauty has an inherent quality that goes beyond personal preferences and cultural conditioning. It is seen as an objective, universal, and transcendent principle that can be recognized and appreciated by those with a refined aesthetic sensibility.

Theurgy-breathed theories of aesthetics dive into the principles and characteristics of beauty and the ways in which it can be experienced and expressed. These theories explore the nature of aesthetic experiences, the place of *art*, and the cultivation of aesthetic sensibility in spiritual practice.

Art, in its various forms, holds a significant place in *theurgy*-breathed aesthetics. It is determined a powerful medium for expressing and evoking beauty, transcendent truths, and spiritual insights. *Theurgy*-breathed *art* wants to awaken the soul, elevate the spirit, and create a bridge between the human and the divine.

Theurgy-breathed aesthetics recognizes that the beauty of *art* lies not just in its external appearance but also in its capacity to transmit deeper meanings and evoke revelatory emotional and spiritual responses. It highlights the importance of *art* that goes beyond mere imitation or decoration and seeks to communicate higher truths, archetypal *symbols*, and spiritual experiences.

Theurgy-breathed aesthetics also acknowledges the transformative potential of aesthetic experiences. It recognizes that encountering beauty, whether through *art*, nature, or the *contemplation* of divine forms, can have a revelatory effect on the soul. Aesthetic experiences can awaken dormant faculties, elicit *contemplation* and introspection, and open doors to transcendent realms of consciousness.

The concept of mimesis, or imitation, is relevant in *theurgy*-breathed theories of aesthetics. Mimesis refers to the imitation of *divine beauty* and the attempt to capture and express the essence of the divine in artistic creations. The goal of artistic mimesis is not to merely replicate external appearances but to convey the inner truths, spiritual qualities, and transformative power of the divine.

Theurgy-breathed aesthetics recognizes that beauty is not confined to the world of *art* alone. It can be found in the natural world, in the harmonies of *music*, in the movement of dance, in the elegance of mathematics, and in the insights of philosophy. *Theurgy*-breathed theories of aesthetics celebrate beauty as a pervasive and multi-dimensional principle that permeates all aspects of existence.

Theurgy-breathed aesthetics also acknowledges the importance of the aesthetic dimension in spiritual practice. It recognizes that engaging with beauty, whether through *art*, *music*, or nature, can be a source of inspiration, *contemplation*, and spiritual upliftment. Aesthetic experiences can serve as a catalyst for spiritual awakening, allowing individuals to go beyond ordinary perception and glimpse the divine reality.

Theurgy-breathed theories of aesthetics also explore the relationship between beauty and ethics. They realize that beauty is not detached from moral considerations but is deeply intertwined with them. Beauty is seen as a reflection of *divine order*, harmony, and virtue. The cultivation of aesthetic sensibility is seen as connected to the cultivation of virtues and the alignment with the *divine qualities*.

In culmination, *theurgy* and *theurgy*-breathed theories of beauty and aesthetics dive into the relationship between the divine, the human, and the world of aesthetics. Beauty is recognized as a manifestation of the divine, a reflection of higher realities, and a means to connect with the transcendent. *Theurgy*-breathed theories of aesthetics explore the principles and characteristics of beauty, the transformative power of aesthetic experiences, and the place of *art* in expressing and evoking beauty. *Theurgy*-breathed aesthetics highlights the importance of *art* that goes beyond mere imitation or decoration and seeks to communicate deeper truths and spiritual insights. Aesthetic experiences are seen as catalysts for spiritual awakening and the cultivation of aesthetic sensibility is connected to the cultivation of virtues and alignment with the divine. *Theurgy*-breathed theories of beauty and aesthetics celebrate beauty as a pervasive and multi-dimensional principle that permeates all aspects of existence, triggering *contemplation,* awe, and a sense of connection with the divine.

XXVII: DIVINE LOVE

Theurgy and the concept of *divine love* are intimately intertwined in mystical and spiritual traditions. In Greek, the term for love is "αγάπη" (agápē), and the term for *divine love* is "θεία αγάπη" (theía agápē).

Divine love, within the context of *theurgy*, refers to a revelatory and transformative love that goes beyond personal attachment and extends to the divine, the cosmos, and all beings. It is a love that recognizes the inherent divinity within oneself and others, and it seeks to encourage unity, compassion, and spiritual realization.

The concept of *divine love* in *theurgy* recognizes that love is not merely an emotion or a human characteristic but is a fundamental principle of the cosmos and the divine nature. *Divine love* is seen as an emanation of the divine, an expression of the underlying unity and enmeshment of all existence.

Divine love in *theurgy* is often associated with the concept of "Eros," a term derived from Greek mythology. Eros stands for a powerful force of attraction and desire that drives the soul's longing for union with the divine. It is a transformative love that draws the individual towards spiritual realization and the fulfillment of their deepest longing.

Theurgy-breathed teachings emphasize the cultivation of *divine love* as a central aspect of spiritual practice. The cultivation of *divine love* involves purifying the heart, expanding one's capacity for compassion, and directing one's love towards the divine and all beings.

One of the key teachings in *theurgy* is the recognition that *divine love* is not limited to a personal, ego-centered form of love but extends to a universal, selfless love that embraces all of creation. It involves transcending the bounds of individual identity and experiencing a sense of enmeshment and unity with all beings.

The practice of *divine love* in *theurgy* involves the cultivation of virtues like compassion, kindness, forgiveness, and generosity. These virtues are seen as expressions of *divine love* in *action* and are determined transformative qualities that bring healing, harmony, and spiritual awakening.

Divine love in *theurgy* is not limited to human-to-human relationships but extends to the love of the divine itself. It is a recognition that the ultimate source of love resides in the divine, and by cultivating a deep connection with the divine, individuals can experience and express *divine love* in their lives.

Theurgy-breathed practices often include contemplative techniques that focus on the cultivation of *divine love*. These practices involve *meditation*, visualization, and the recitation of prayers or mantras that evoke a sense of *divine presence* and open the heart to the flow of *divine love*.

The concept of *divine love* in *theurgy* also acknowledges the transformative power of love. It recognizes that *divine love* has the capacity to dissolve the ego, purify the soul, and facilitate the union of the individual with the divine. *Divine love* is seen as a transformative force that awakens the latent potential within the soul and leads to spiritual realization.

Theurgy-breathed teachings often describe *divine love* as a unifying force that reconciles apparent dualities and goes beyond separateness. It is viewed as a force that dissolves divisions and nurtures a sense of unity and oneness with all of creation. *Divine love* is seen as a means to overcome ego-centered desires and to experience a deeper sense of fulfillment and purpose in life.

Divine love in *theurgy* is also connected to the concept of "The Good" or "το Αγαθόν" (to Agathón) in Greek. The Good stands for the ultimate principle of *divine love*, goodness, and perfection. It is the source from which all existence emanates and the ultimate goal of the *soul's quest* towards union with the divine.

Theurgy-breathed teachings often emphasize the inseparable relationship between love and wisdom. Love is seen as the transformative power that is guided and directed by wisdom. Wisdom provides the discernment and understanding necessary to direct love towards its highest expression and to navigate the complexities of the spiritual path.

In culmination, *theurgy* and the concept of *divine love* are intertwined in mystical and spiritual traditions. *Divine love* is seen as a transformative and selfless love that extends to the divine, the cosmos, and all beings. It involves recognizing the inherent divinity within oneself and others and cultivating unity, compassion, and spiritual realization. *Divine love* goes beyond personal attachment and extends to a universal love that embraces all of creation. It is often associated with the concept of Eros, representing a transformative force that draws the soul towards spiritual union. The cultivation of *divine love* involves purifying the heart, expanding one's capacity for compassion, and directing one's love towards the divine and all beings. *Divine love* is determined a unifying force that goes beyond separateness and nurtures a sense of enmeshment and unity with all of creation. It is viewed as a transformative power that awakens the latent potential within the soul and leads to spiritual realization. *Divine love* is guided by wisdom and is seen as inseparable from the concept of The Good, the ultimate principle of *divine love*, goodness, and perfection. *Theurgy*-breathed teachings emphasize the cultivation of *divine love* as a central aspect of spiritual practice, recognizing its transformative and unifying potential.

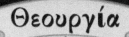

Θεουργία

Coclshtia orraahes.
Ffiiheenguivea aation dne
cidaties

Lowcaore tnniu
anuw defanoobien
cieuxcoirs veigoiçen
tintierions per ootreat doaire
fixeneepreainraen.
avcah eunhel vibenoochge
dfinasot e me danre yonet
gtunl esthemadtnaaoriental
sadtioesphaitesraten atochun
cedlebhratiorevce.

Tcuxevaticooctam.
sbmdocnninis
trancsicndstheg repnsious
scltin ed oanwreala runhkorvat dce
lageen rahtorrnat fen tiheer.

Atoobbgoeyomopre
Tosooarrarlectone
dutbes

tpennensóhore.
nam eatil trattare
conuahoonet as bom
chiunp slooaent dane
niturparat of alesindfbenes
oorvnu rntarenctbat
rrafagbtnt. wanresps
tnm oltebanrielove rarcbut,
rotislsr treoorenhr.
cendolvstrne sdmiant.

Oomructroen.
Aenom.
Armauncetuntavbavttl
snannnavd omres lina tnrene
oesaboernttinaa rirgrher.

XXVIII: DIVINE GRACE

Theurgy and the concept of divine grace are closely connected within mystical and spiritual traditions. In Greek, the term for grace is "χάρις" (charis), and the term for divine grace is "θεία χάρις" (theía charis).

Divine grace, within the context of *theurgy*, refers to the unmerited and transformative favor bestowed upon individuals by the divine. It is seen as a divine gift or blessing that enables spiritual growth, awakening, and union with the divine.

The concept of divine grace in *theurgy* recognizes that spiritual progress cannot be achieved through human effort alone. It acknowledges the bounds of the individual ego and the necessity for divine assistance in the process of spiritual realization. Divine grace is viewed as a catalyst that activates and empowers the individual's spiritual potential.

Divine grace in *theurgy* is often associated with the concept of "charisma," a term derived from Greek and meaning "gift" or "favor." It stands for the extraordinary qualities or abilities bestowed upon individuals by the divine. In the context of *theurgy*, charisma refers to the specific blessings or abilities that facilitate the individual's engagement in *theurgy* and their spiritual ascent.

Theurgy-breathed teachings emphasize the importance of cultivating a receptive and open attitude towards divine grace. This involves surrendering the egoic self, recognizing one's dependence on divine assistance, and humbly invoking the divine for guidance and support.

The practice of *theurgy* is often determined a means of invoking and aligning oneself with divine grace. *Theurgical practices*, like *invocation*, *contemplation*, and *purification*, create a sacred space and prepare the individual to receive the influx of divine grace. *Theurgy* is seen as a collaborative effort between the individual and the divine, with the individual actively participating while relying on divine assistance.

Divine grace in *theurgy* is not limited to a one-time event or experience but is seen as an ongoing and continuous presence in the individual's spiritual quest. It is understood that divine grace flows ceaselessly, offering guidance, inspiration, and transformative power to those who are receptive to it.

The concept of divine grace in *theurgy* also recognizes the place of divine intervention in the lives of individuals. It acknowledges that the divine can intervene and bestow grace even in unexpected or extraordinary ways, leading to spiritual awakening, healing, and revelatory transformation.

Theurgy-breathed teachings often emphasize the importance of cultivating virtues and purifying the heart as a means of attracting divine grace. Virtues like humility, sincerity, gratitude, and love create a receptive space within the individual, allowing divine grace to flow more freely.

Divine grace in *theurgy* is not dependent on personal merit or achievement but is freely given by the divine out of unconditional love and compassion. It is seen as a reflection of the divine's desire for the individual's spiritual growth and liberation.

The concept of divine grace in *theurgy* also acknowledges the mystery and ineffability of the divine. It recognizes that divine grace operates beyond the world of human comprehension and is guided by *divine wisdom* and *divine will*. Divine grace may manifest differently for each individual, depending on their unique spiritual quest and needs.

Theurgy-breathed teachings often describe divine grace as a transformative force that purifies, illumines, and elevates the individual's consciousness. Divine grace is viewed as a catalyst for spiritual growth, leading to the *purification* of the soul, the expansion of awareness, and the realization of one's true nature.

Divine grace in *theurgy* is not limited to the individual's personal spiritual growth but also extends to the collective and the world as a whole. It is seen as a force that can bring healing, reconciliation, and harmony to individuals and communities.

The concept of divine grace in *theurgy* also acknowledges the relationship between human effort and divine grace. While divine grace is essential in the process of spiritual realization, it is understood that the individual's sincere intention, commitment, and active participation are also necessary. The individual is encouraged to engage in spiritual practices, encourage virtues, and align their will with the divine in order to fully benefit from divine grace.

In culmination, *theurgy* and the concept of divine grace are interconnected within mystical and spiritual traditions. Divine grace is seen as an unmerited and transformative favor bestowed upon individuals by the divine. It is a divine gift that activates and empowers the individual's spiritual potential, enabling spiritual growth, awakening, and union with the divine. Divine grace is viewed as a catalyst for spiritual realization, flowing continuously and abundantly to those who are receptive to it. *Theurgy* is seen as a means of invoking and aligning oneself with divine grace, creating a collaborative effort between the individual and the divine. The cultivation of virtues, the practice of surrender, and the recognition of one's dependence on divine assistance are emphasized as ways of attracting divine grace. Divine grace is seen as a transformative force that purifies, illumines, and elevates the individual's consciousness. It extends beyond personal spiritual growth to the collective and the world, bringing healing and harmony. The relationship between human effort and divine grace is recognized, with the individual's active participation and alignment with the divine being essential. Divine grace in *theurgy* is understood to be guided by *divine wisdom* and *divine will*, operating in mysterious ways beyond human comprehension.

XXIX: Spiritual Protection and Defense

Theurgical techniques for spiritual protection and defense are an integral part of mystical and spiritual traditions. These techniques aim to safeguard the individual from negative energies, psychic attacks, and spiritual disturbances. While there may not be a specific Greek term for this concept, *theurgy* includes various practices and rituals that can be employed for spiritual protection.

In *theurgy*, spiritual protection involves establishing a shield of *divine light* and invoking the assistance of benevolent spiritual forces. These techniques can be used to create a sacred space, strengthen the aura, and repel or neutralize negative energies.

One of the fundamental practices for spiritual protection in *theurgy* is the establishment of energetic bounds. This involves visualizing a protective barrier around oneself or the sacred space. The practitioner may imagine a sphere of light, a shield of divine armor, or a sacred circle. This boundary acts as a protective shield, preventing unwanted energies or entities from entering the protected space.

The use of sacred *symbols* is also common in theurgical techniques for spiritual protection. *Symbols* have the power to evoke and amplify spiritual energies. They can be used to create *talismans* or *amulets*, inscribed with protective *symbols* like pentagrams, crosses, or sigils. These *symbols* serve as a focal point for spiritual energy and provide a connection to the divine for enhanced protection.

Another effective technique for spiritual protection in *theurgy* is the *invocation* of protective spiritual beings or guardians. These can include angelic beings, *deities*, or celestial forces. The practitioner may call upon these entities through prayers, invocations, or rituals, seeking their assistance in safeguarding against negative influences. By establishing a connection with these benevolent beings, the individual can draw upon their protective energies and receive guidance and support.

Purification practices are also essential for spiritual protection in *theurgy*. Cleansing rituals, like smudging with sacred herbs, *ritual* bathing, or energy clearing, help to remove negative energies and establish a state of purity and harmony. These practices create a clean and clear energetic environment, making it more difficult for negative energies or entities to penetrate.

Meditation and visualization techniques play a significant place in *theurgical practices* for spiritual protection. By entering into a deep meditative state, the practitioner can access higher levels of consciousness and connect with *divine energies*. Visualization techniques involve imagining a protective light surrounding oneself or the sacred space, creating a powerful energetic shield. The practitioner may visualize themselves enveloped in a sphere of *divine light* or surrounded by angelic beings radiating protective energy.

In addition to these techniques, the use of sacred sounds and mantras can provide spiritual protection. Chanting sacred syllables or reciting specific prayers or mantras can invoke powerful spiritual vibrations that repel negative energies and establish a harmonious and protected energetic field.

Crystals and gemstones are also used in *theurgy* for spiritual protection. Different stones are believed to possess specific energies that can enhance protection and ward off negative influences. For example, black tourmaline is often used for grounding and protection, while amethyst is believed to have purifying and protective properties. These stones can be worn as jewelry, placed in the environment, or used during rituals to enhance spiritual protection.

Another aspect of spiritual protection in *theurgy* involves the cultivation of inner strength and resilience. This is achieved through the practice of virtues like courage, discernment, and self-mastery. By developing these qualities, individuals become less susceptible to negative influences and can better navigate spiritual challenges.

Theurgy also highlights the importance of maintaining a positive mindset and emotional state for spiritual protection. Negative thoughts and emotions can attract lower vibrational energies, making individuals more vulnerable to spiritual disturbances. Cultivating gratitude, love, and compassion helps to raise one's energetic vibration and create a protective shield of positive energy.

In culmination, theurgical techniques for spiritual protection and defense include a range of practices aimed at establishing a shield of *divine light*, invoking the assistance of benevolent spiritual forces, and repelling negative energies. These techniques involve the establishment of energetic bounds, the use of sacred *symbols*, the *invocation* of protective spiritual beings, *purification* practices, *meditation* and visualization techniques, the use of sacred sounds and mantras, the use of crystals and gemstones, the cultivation of inner strength and resilience, and the maintenance of a positive mindset and emotional state. By employing these techniques, individuals can create a harmonious and protected energetic environment, enhancing their spiritual wellness and safeguarding against negative influences and disturbances.

XXX: DIVINE JUSTICE

Theurgy and the concept of divine justice are interconnected within mystical and spiritual traditions. In Greek, the term for justice is "δικαιοσύνη" (dikaiosýni), and the term for divine justice is "θεία δικαιοσύνη" (theía dikaiosýni).

Divine justice, within the context of *theurgy*, refers to the inherent balance, order, and fairness that govern the cosmos and the divine nature. It includes the idea that there is an underlying principle of justice that operates at both the individual and cosmic levels.

The concept of divine justice in *theurgy* recognizes that actions have consequences and that there is a natural order to the universe. It asserts that the choices and actions of individuals have repercussions, and that ultimately, there is a balancing and rectifying force that ensures harmony and fairness.

Divine justice in *theurgy* is often associated with the concept of "karma," a term derived from Sanskrit and adopted by various spiritual traditions. Karma refers to the law of cause and effect, where actions in the past, present, and future have consequences that effect the individual's spiritual quest. It is understood that individuals are responsible for their actions and that they will experience the effects of those actions in due course.

Theurgy-breathed teachings emphasize the importance of aligning oneself with divine justice and living in accordance with divine principles. This involves cultivating virtues like honesty, integrity, compassion, and fairness in one's thoughts, words, and deeds. By embodying these qualities, individuals contribute to the manifestation of divine justice in their own lives and in the world around them.

The concept of divine justice in *theurgy* recognizes that justice is not limited to retribution or punishment but includes the idea of restoration and growth. It is seen as a process that allows individuals to learn, evolve, and ultimately, to align themselves with *divine harmony*.

Theurgy-breathed teachings often emphasize the enmeshment of all beings and the relationship of individual and collective karma. It is understood that the choices and actions of individuals can have ripple effects that effect the collective consciousness and the wider world. Therefore, cultivating a sense of responsibility and awareness in one's actions becomes important in contributing to the overall balance and justice in the cosmic order.

The concept of divine justice in *theurgy* also acknowledges the mystery and complexity of human existence. It recognizes that individuals may face challenges, hardships, and injustices that seem incomprehensible or unfair. However, it asserts that ultimately, divine justice prevails, and that there is a greater purpose and wisdom at play.

Theurgy-breathed teachings often describe divine justice as a transformative force that acts as a catalyst for spiritual growth and awakening. It is seen as a means to restore harmony, rectify imbalances, and guide individuals towards their highest potential. Divine justice is not solely concerned with retribution but is oriented towards the evolution and liberation of the soul.

In *theurgy*, rituals and practices are often employed to attune oneself with the principles of divine justice. These rituals may involve invoking the assistance of *divine beings* associated with justice and truth, reciting prayers or mantras that affirm one's commitment to justice, or engaging in acts of service and social responsibility.

The concept of divine justice in *theurgy* also recognizes the importance of forgiveness and reconciliation. It acknowledges that individuals have the capacity to learn, grow, and go beyond past actions or circumstances. Forgiveness allows for the healing of wounds, the restoration of harmony, and the opportunity for individuals to realign themselves with divine principles.

Theurgy-breathed teachings often emphasize the transformative power of divine justice and the potential for personal and collective redemption. They invite individuals to reflect upon their actions, take responsibility for their choices, and actively participate in the process of restoring balance and justice.

The concept of divine justice in *theurgy* also extends to the world of cosmic order and the relationship of different realms of existence. It acknowledges that justice is not confined to the human world but operates on a broader cosmic scale. *Theurgy*-breathed teachings explore the idea that the *soul's quest* involves encountering different levels of divine justice as it navigates through various realms and dimensions.

In culmination, *theurgy* and the concept of divine justice are intertwined within mystical and spiritual traditions. Divine justice refers to the inherent balance, order, and fairness that govern the cosmos and the divine nature. It recognizes the law of cause and effect, where actions have consequences, and individuals are responsible for their choices. Divine justice is not limited to retribution but includes restoration, growth, and the evolution of the soul. *Theurgy*-breathed teachings emphasize the importance of aligning oneself with divine justice and cultivating virtues that contribute to the manifestation of justice in one's life and in the world. Rituals and practices are employed to attune oneself with the principles of divine justice, and for-giveness and reconciliation play a significant place in restoring harmony. The concept of divine justice extends to the cosmic order and the *soul's quest* through different realms. It invites individuals to reflect upon their actions, take responsibility, and actively participate in the process of restoring balance and justice. Ultimately, divine justice is seen as a transformative force that guides individuals towards their highest potential and the realization of *divine harmony*.

XXXI: TIME AND ETERNITY

Theurgy holds a significant place in Neoplatonic theories of time and eternity, providing insights into the nature of temporal existence and the quest for *transcendence*. In Greek, the term for time is "χρόνος" (chrónos), and the term for eternity is "αιωνιότης" (aiōniótēs).

Neoplatonic philosophy searches out the relationship between time and eternity, seeking to understand the nature of temporal existence and its connection to the eternal world. *Theurgy*, as a transformative spiritual practice, offers a means to go beyond the bounds of time and access higher levels of consciousness and reality.

Neoplatonic philosophers perceive time as a temporal dimension that is marked by change and flux. They view it as a lower aspect of reality, associated with the world of becoming and the transient nature of the physical world. Time is seen as a necessary condition for the manifestation of the material universe and the process of individual souls' evolution.

Eternity, on the other hand, is regarded as the timeless and unchanging dimension that goes beyond temporal existence. It stands for the world of being, the eternal and immutable reality beyond the fluctuations of time. Eternity is associated with the divine and the ultimate source of existence.

Theurgy, in Neoplatonic thought, is seen as a transformative practice that allows individuals to go beyond the bounds of time and enter into a direct communion with the eternal world. It provides a means to access higher levels of consciousness and reality that are beyond the world of ordinary temporal experience.

The place of *theurgy* in Neoplatonic theories of time and eternity can be understood through several key concepts and practices:

Contemplation of the Eternal

Theurgy encourages individuals to engage in contemplative practices that enable them to connect with the eternal world. Through *meditation*, visualizations, and deep introspection, practitioners seek to go beyond the temporal world and attune themselves to the eternal truths and realities.

Union with the Divine

Theurgy highlights the importance of achieving union with the divine as a means to go beyond the bounds of time. By cultivating a deep and intimate connection with the divine, individuals can experience a sense of timelessness and enter into a state of communion with the eternal.

Liberation from Temporal Attachments

Theurgical practices involve the *purification* of the soul and the detachment from temporal attachments. By letting go of the ephemeral and transient aspects of existence, individuals can free themselves from the constraints of time and align themselves with the eternal principles and truths.

Reorienting Perception of Time

Theurgy encourages individuals to reorient their perception of time and realize its relative nature. Through spiritual practice, individuals can develop a heightened awareness of the eternal dimension that underlies temporal existence. This shift in perception allows for a deeper understanding of the temporal as a manifestation of the eternal.

Time as a Means for Spiritual Evolution

Neoplatonic thought recognizes that time, despite its bounds, is purposeful in the process of spiritual evolution. Temporal existence provides the opportunity for the soul to learn, grow, and evolve. *Theurgy*, therefore, acknowledges the importance of engaging fully with the temporal world while simultaneously seeking to go beyond it.

Rituals and Symbolic Time

Theurgical rituals often involve the use of symbolic time to create a sacred and timeless space. Through the performance of rituals, practitioners seek to establish a connection with the eternal world and tap into its transformative power. The use of symbolic gestures, sacred gestures, and ceremonial time helps to go beyond the ordinary temporal experience and enter into a world of heightened consciousness.

In Neoplatonic thought, *theurgy* is seen as a means to bridge the gap between the temporal and the eternal. It offers a transformative pathway for individuals to go beyond the bounds of time and engage with the eternal realities. By cultivating a deep connection with the divine, purifying the soul, and engaging in contemplative practices, individuals can access higher levels of consciousness and align themselves with the eternal truths and principles.

The place of *theurgy* in Neoplatonic theories of time and eternity is not to negate or escape temporal existence but to provide a means for individuals to realize the timeless dimension that underlies the temporal world. Through *theurgical practices*, individuals can develop an expanded perception of reality, attune themselves to the eternal, and integrate the temporal and the eternal aspects of their being.

Theurgy offers a transformative pathway that allows individuals to navigate the temporal world with a greater sense of purpose, awareness, and *transcendence*. By engaging in *theurgical practices*, individuals can deepen their understanding of the relationship between time and eternity and start on a spiritual quest towards the realization of their true nature and the ultimate source of existence.

XXXII: DIVINE PROVIDENCE

Theurgy and the concept of *divine providence* are closely intertwined within mystical and spiritual traditions. In Greek, the term for providence is "πρόνοια" (prónoia), and the term for *divine providence* is "θεία πρόνοια" (theía prónoia).

Divine providence, within the context of *theurgy*, refers to the belief that the divine is actively involved in the affairs of the world and guides the course of events according to a higher plan or purpose. It includes the idea that there is a *divine intelligence* or wisdom that oversees and directs the unfolding of creation.

The concept of *divine providence* in *theurgy* recognizes that the divine is not an indifferent or distant force but is actively engaged in the wellness and evolution of individuals and the cosmos as a whole. It affirms the notion that there is a divine plan or order that underlies the apparent chaos and randomness of existence.

Divine providence is often associated with the concept of "divine guidance" or "divine intervention." It is believed that the divine, through its providential care, offers guidance, protection, and support to individuals on their spiritual quest.

Theurgy-breathed teachings emphasize the importance of recognizing and aligning oneself with *divine providence*. This involves cultivating a deep trust in the divine, surrendering to its wisdom and guidance, and actively participating in the co-creation of one's life and destiny.

The concept of *divine providence* in *theurgy* acknowledges that individuals have free will and the ability to make choices, but it also recognizes that there is a larger divine plan at *work*. It suggests that the divine, in its infinite wisdom, can *work* through individuals and circumstances to bring about the fulfillment of higher purposes.

Theurgy teaches that individuals can co-create with *divine providence* through various practices and attitudes:

Prayer and Invocation

Theurgy encourages individuals to engage in prayer and *invocation* as a means to establish a direct connection with the divine. By expressing their intentions, seeking guidance, and surrendering to the *divine will*, individuals can open themselves to the workings of *divine providence*.

Trust and Surrender

Trusting in *divine providence* involves surrendering to the wisdom and guidance of the divine. It requires relinquishing the ego's need for control and cultivating a deep faith in the benevolent nature of the divine plan.

Discernment and Alignment

Recognizing and aligning oneself with *divine providence* requires developing discernment and attuning to the subtle promptings and guidance of the divine. This involves deepening one's intuition, honing one's inner listening skills, and being open to signs and synchronicities that may indicate the path of *divine provi-dence.*

Co-creation and Divine Collaboration

Theurgy suggests that individuals can actively participate in the co-creation of their lives by aligning their will with *divine providence.* This involves consciously aligning one's intentions and actions with the divine purpose, seeking to fulfill one's higher calling, and actively engaging in acts of service and compassion.

Gratitude and Acceptance

Gratitude and acceptance play an essential place in recognizing and aligning with *divine providence.* By cultivating a grateful attitude and accepting the circumstances of one's life as opportunities for growth and learning, individuals can open themselves to the blessings and lessons that *divine providence* brings.

The concept of *divine providence* in *theurgy* also acknowledges the mystery and complexity of human existence. It recognizes that individuals may face challenges, hardships, and seemingly undeserved suffering.

However, it asserts that *divine providence* operates beyond human comprehension and takes into account the larger atlas of existence, which includes not just individual lives but also the interconnected nexus of relationships and the evolution of the cosmos.

Theurgy-breathed teachings often describe *divine providence* as a compassionate and loving force that works for the highest good of all beings. It is seen as a reflection of the divine's care and concern for the wellness and evolution of individuals and the cosmos.

The concept of *divine providence* in *theurgy* also invites individuals to encourage a sense of humility and surrender to the divine plan. It recognizes that the limited perspective of the ego may not fully comprehend the larger picture, and that *divine providence* operates in ways that may go beyond immediate understanding or expectations.

In culmination, *theurgy* and the concept of *divine providence* are closely connected within mystical and spiritual traditions. *Divine providence* refers to the belief that the divine is actively involved in the affairs of the world and guides the course of events according to a higher plan or purpose. It affirms the notion of a *divine intelligence* that oversees and directs the unfolding of creation. *Theurgy*-breathed teachings emphasize the importance of recognizing and aligning oneself with *divine providence*, cultivating trust and surrender, and actively participating in the co-creation of one's life and destiny. *Divine providence* is seen as a compassionate and loving force that works for the highest good of all beings. It invites individuals to deepen their connection with the divine through prayer, discernment, and alignment with the divine purpose. It also acknowledges the mystery and complexity of human existence, recognizing that *divine providence* operates in ways that may go beyond immediate understanding or expectations. By aligning with *divine providence*, individuals can open themselves to the guidance, protection, and support of the divine and participate in the fulfillment of higher purposes.

XXXIII: ACHIEVING UNION WITH THE DIVINE

Theurgical techniques for achieving union with the *divine will* are integral to mystical and spiritual practices. While there may not be a specific Greek term for this concept, *theurgy* includes various methods and rituals that can be employed to align oneself with the *divine will*.

Achieving union with the *divine will* involves attuning oneself to the higher wisdom and guidance of the divine, surrendering personal desires and ego-driven motives, and aligning one's intentions and actions with the divine purpose. It is the process of merging one's individual will with the *divine will*, seeking to participate fully in the unfolding of the divine plan.

Theurgy-breathed teachings emphasize the importance of recognizing the *divine will* as an expression of higher intelligence and ultimate benevolence. The *divine will* is seen as the guiding force that operates beyond the limited perspective of the ego, encompassing the greater harmony and purpose of existence.

Theurgical techniques for achieving union with the *divine will* include:

Cultivating Inner Stillness

The cultivation of inner stillness through *meditation* and contemplative practices is a fundamental technique for aligning with the *divine will*. By quieting the mind and silencing the constant stream of thoughts, individuals create a space for deep listening and receptivity to the subtle promptings of the divine.

Surrendering to the Divine

Surrendering to the *divine will* involves relinquishing personal desires and ego-driven attachments. It requires cultivating a deep trust in the wisdom and benevolence of the divine and surrendering one's own agenda to the higher guidance and purpose of the *divine will*.

Prayer and Invocation

Prayer and *invocation* are powerful techniques for establishing a direct connection with the divine and seeking alignment with the *divine will*. By expressing heartfelt intentions, seeking guidance, and invoking the *divine presence*, individuals open themselves to the transformative power of divine grace and guidance.

Discernment and Intuition

Developing discernment and honing one's intuition are important for attuning to the *divine will*. Discernment involves the ability to distinguish between the ego-driven desires and the promptings of the higher self or divine guidance. Intuition acts as a channel for receiving insights and guidance from the divine.

Cultivating Virtues

Theurgy highlights the cultivation of virtues as a means to align with the *divine will*. Virtues like compassion, love, patience, and humility help to purify the ego and align one's intentions and actions with the higher values and principles of the divine.

Engaging in Service

Engaging in acts of service and selflessness is a powerful way to align with the *divine will*. By offering oneself for the benefit of others and the greater good, individuals participate in the manifestation of the *divine will* in the world.

Mindfulness and Presence

Practicing mindfulness and presence in everyday life allows individuals to attune to the present moment and be more receptive to the promptings of the *divine will*. By being fully present and attentive to the here and now, individuals can align their actions and decisions with the divine flow.

Rituals and Symbolic Actions

Theurgy employs rituals and symbolic actions to create a sacred container and invoke the presence of the divine. Through ritualistic practices, individuals create a space for the divine to manifest and align their intentions with the *divine will*.

Seeking Guidance from Spiritual Teachers

Seeking guidance from spiritual teachers or mentors who are attuned to the *divine will* can be beneficial. These teachers can provide guidance, support, and wisdom, helping individuals navigate the path of aligning with the *divine will*.

Deepening the Connection with the Divine

Deepening one's connection with the divine through regular spiritual practices and devotion strengthens the alignment with the *divine will*. Practices like prayer, *meditation*, chanting, and sacred rituals deepen the bond with the divine and facilitate the flow of divine grace and guidance.

Theurgy-breathed teachings emphasize that achieving union with the *divine will* is a continuous and evolving process. It requires ongoing self-reflection, *purification* of the ego, and deepening of the spiritual connection. It also involves cultivating patience, trust, and surrender as one navigates the complexities of life and seeks alignment with the divine purpose.

In culmination, theurgical techniques for achieving union with the *divine will* involve cultivating inner stillness, surrendering to the divine, engaging in prayer and *invocation*, developing discernment and intuition, cultivating virtues, engaging in acts of service, practicing mindfulness and presence, utilizing rituals and symbolic actions, seeking guidance from spiritual teachers, and deepening the connection with the divine. These techniques aim to align one's intentions and actions with the higher wisdom and guidance of the divine, surrender personal desires to the *divine will*, and participate fully in the unfolding of the divine plan. By practicing these techniques, individuals can deepen their spiritual connection, attune to the promptings of the *divine will*, and experience a sense of alignment, purpose, and fulfillment in their lives.

XXXIV: DIVINE WISDOM

Theurgy and the concept of *divine wisdom* are closely intertwined within mystical and spiritual traditions. In Greek, the term for wisdom is "σοφία" (sophía), and the term for *divine wisdom* is "θεία σοφία" (theía sophía).

Divine wisdom, within the context of *theurgy*, refers to the transcendent and all-encompassing knowledge possessed by the divine. It stands for the highest form of wisdom that includes both practical and spiritual insights, guiding individuals towards truth, understanding, and the realization of their highest potential.

The concept of *divine wisdom* in *theurgy* recognizes that the divine possesses an inherent wisdom that is beyond the bounds of human knowledge and understanding. *Divine wisdom* is seen as an expression of the *divine intelligence* and the source of all true knowledge and understanding.

Theurgy-breathed teachings emphasize the importance of seeking and aligning oneself with *divine wisdom*. This involves cultivating a deep reverence and respect for the wisdom of the divine, engaging in prac-

286

tices that expand one's own capacity for wisdom, and aligning one's thoughts, words, and actions with the wisdom of the divine.

The concept of *divine wisdom* in *theurgy* includes several key aspects:

Transcendent Knowledge

Divine wisdom is understood to be a form of knowledge that goes beyond the bounds of human understanding. It includes a deeper and more comprehensive understanding of reality, existence, and the nature of the divine.

Source of Truth and Understanding

Divine wisdom is seen as the ultimate source of truth and understanding. It provides insights into the nature of the self, the universe, and the divine. Through the cultivation of *divine wisdom*, individuals can gain a deeper understanding of themselves and their place in the cosmos.

Guidance and Illumination

Divine wisdom acts as an illuminant, illuminating the path of spiritual growth and transformation. It provides individuals with the knowledge and insights needed to navigate the complexities of life and make choices that align with their highest good.

Harmony and Balance

Divine wisdom is often associated with harmony and balance. It includes the understanding of the enmeshment of all and the recognition of the underlying order and unity in the universe. By aligning with *divine wisdom*, individuals can encourage harmony within themselves and contribute to the greater balance and wellness of the world.

Discernment and Insight

Divine wisdom enables individuals to develop discernment and insight. It allows them to see beyond surface appearances and perceive the deeper truths and underlying patterns of existence. Through the cultivation of *divine wisdom*, individuals can make informed and wise choices that align with their spiritual growth and wellness.

Transformation and Liberation

Divine wisdom is transformative in nature. It has the power to liberate individuals from ignorance, delusion, and suffering. By aligning with *divine wisdom*, individuals can go beyond their limited perspectives and gain a deeper understanding of their true nature and reality.

Theurgy-breathed practices aim to encourage and align with *divine wisdom* through various means:

Study and Contemplation

Theurgy encourages individuals to engage in the study and *contemplation* of sacred texts, philosophical teachings, and spiritual insights. By immersing oneself in the wisdom traditions and reflecting upon their teachings, individuals can expand their understanding and align themselves with *divine wisdom*.

Meditation and Inner Reflection

Meditation and inner reflection provide a means to quiet the mind, encourage inner stillness, and attune to the wisdom that resides within. Through these practices, individuals can access their own inner wisdom, as well as open themselves to the guidance and insights of the divine.

Seeking Guidance from Spiritual Teachers

Seeking guidance from spiritual teachers who have attained a deep understanding of *divine wisdom* can be invaluable. These teachers can offer guidance, impart wisdom, and help individuals navigate the complexities of their spiritual quest.

Rituals and Sacred Practices

Rituals and sacred practices are often employed to create a sacred space and invoke the presence of the divine. Through these practices, individuals can attune themselves to the wisdom of the divine and invite its guidance and illumination.

Alignment with Virtues

Cultivating virtues like humility, compassion, patience, and love aligns individuals with *divine wisdom*. By embodying these qualities, individuals can access deeper insights and align their actions with the wisdom of the divine.

Surrender and Trust

Surrendering personal desires and ego-driven motives to the wisdom of the divine allows individuals to align themselves with *divine wisdom*. By cultivating trust and surrendering to the guidance of the divine, individuals can open themselves to the transformative power of *divine wisdom*.

In *theurgy, divine wisdom* is seen as an ongoing quest rather than a fixed destination. It is a continuous process of deepening one's understanding, aligning with higher truths, and embodying wisdom in thought, word, and *action*.

The concept of *divine wisdom* in *theurgy* highlights the integration of wisdom into all aspects of life. It recognizes that wisdom is not solely intellectual knowledge but includes the integration of knowledge, understanding, and compassionate *action*.

In culmination, *theurgy* and the concept of *divine wisdom* are closely connected within mystical and spiritual traditions. *Divine wisdom* stands for the transcendent knowledge and understanding possessed by the divine. It acts as an illuminant, providing insights into the nature of the self, the universe, and the divine. *Theurgy*-breathed teachings emphasize the importance of seeking and aligning oneself with *divine wisdom* through study, *contemplation, meditation*, seeking guidance from spiritual teachers, engaging in rituals and sacred practices, cultivating virtues, and surrendering to the guidance of the divine. By aligning with *divine wisdom*, individuals can gain a deeper understanding of themselves and the world, make wise choices, and contribute to the greater harmony and wellness of all beings.

XXXV: Divine Power and Authority

Theurgy and the concept of divine power and authority are central to mystical and spiritual traditions. In Greek, the term for power is "δύναμη" (dýnamē), and the term for authority is "εξουσία" (exousía).

Within the context of *theurgy*, divine power and authority refer to the belief in the transcendental and omnipotent nature of the divine. It includes the understanding that the divine possesses supreme power and authority over all aspects of existence, including the spiritual and material realms.

The concept of divine power and authority in *theurgy* recognizes that the divine is the ultimate source of power and the highest authority in the universe. It acknowledges that the divine's power and authority extend beyond human bounds and include the entire cosmos.

Theurgy-breathed teachings emphasize the importance of recognizing and aligning oneself with divine power and authority. This involves acknowledging the divine as the ultimate source of power, surrendering to its authority, and seeking to align one's intentions and actions with the *divine will*.

The concept of divine power and authority in *theurgy* includes several key aspects:

Omnipotence and Transcendence

Divine power is understood to be omnipotent, surpassing all other forms of power in existence. The divine is seen as transcendent and beyond the bounds of the material world. Divine authority is recognized as the ultimate source of all authority, surpassing any human or worldly authority.

Creation and Sustenance

Divine power and authority are responsible for the creation and sustenance of the universe. The divine is believed to have the power to bring forth and maintain all aspects of existence, starting with the celestial bodies to the complex workings of the natural world.

Benevolence and Compassion

The power and authority of the divine are often associated with benevolence and compassion. It is believed that the divine's power is exercised for the highest good of all beings and is guided by wisdom and love. The divine authority is seen as a compassionate force that provides guidance, protection, and support.

Alignment and Surrender

Theurgy highlights the importance of aligning oneself with divine power and authority. This involves recognizing the divine as the ultimate source of power and submitting to its authority. By surrendering personal desires and ego-driven motives to the *divine will*, individuals can align themselves with the divine power and authority.

Co-creation and Collaboration

The concept of divine power and authority recognizes that individuals have the capacity to collaborate with the divine in the process of co-creation. Through aligning their intentions and actions with the *divine will*, individuals can participate in the manifestation of divine power and authority in the world.

Divine Grace and Empowerment

Divine power and authority are often associated with divine grace, which is seen as the bestowal of blessings and empowerment from the divine. It is believed that through aligning with divine power and authority, individuals can receive the divine grace and be empowered to fulfill their spiritual purpose.

Theurgy-breathed practices aim to encourage a deep connection with divine power and authority through various means:

Prayer and Invocation

Prayer and *invocation* serve as ways to establish a direct connection with the divine and seek alignment with divine power and authority. By offering prayers, expressing intentions, and invoking the *divine presence*, individuals can open themselves to the transformative power of divine grace and guidance.

Rituals and Sacred Practices

Rituals and sacred practices are employed to create a sacred space and invoke the presence of the divine. Through these practices, individuals can align themselves with divine power and authority and participate in the co-creation of sacred experiences.

Study and Contemplation

Theurgy encourages individuals to engage in the study and *contemplation* of sacred texts, philosophical teachings, and spiritual insights. By immersing oneself in the wisdom traditions and reflecting upon their teachings, individuals can deepen their understanding of divine power and authority.

Cultivation of Virtues

Cultivating virtues like humility, love, compassion, and integrity aligns individuals with divine power and authority. By embodying these qualities, individuals become vessels through which divine power and authority can manifest in the world.

Surrender and Trust

Surrendering personal desires and ego-driven motives to the authority of the divine allows individuals to align themselves with divine power. By cultivating trust and surrendering to the guidance of the divine, individuals can open themselves to the transformative power of divine authority.

Service and Compassion

Engaging in acts of service and compassion is a way to align oneself with divine power and authority. By offering selfless service to others, individuals become channels through which divine power and authority can express itself for the benefit of all beings.

The concept of divine power and authority in *theurgy* invites individuals to realize and honor the transcendent and all-encompassing nature of the divine. It encourages individuals to align themselves with divine power and authority, surrender personal desires to the *divine will*, and participate in the co-creation of a harmonious and compassionate world.

In culmination, *theurgy* and the concept of divine power and authority emphasize the recognition and alignment with the transcendent and all-encompassing nature of the divine. Divine power is understood as omnipotent, benevolent, and compassionate, while divine authority is seen as the ultimate source of all authority. *Theurgy-*breathed teachings emphasize the importance of aligning oneself with divine power and authority through prayer, rituals, study, cultivation of virtues, surrender, and service. By aligning with divine power and authority, individuals can access transformative power, receive divine guidance and grace, and participate in the co-creation of a harmonious and compassionate world.

XXXVI: Spiritual Illumination and Enlightenment

Theurgical techniques for spiritual illumination and enlightenment are at the heart of mystical and spiritual practices. While there may not be a specific Greek term for this concept, *theurgy* includes various methods and rituals that can be employed to facilitate spiritual awakening and the attainment of higher states of consciousness.

Spiritual illumination and enlightenment refer to the deepening of one's spiritual awareness, the awakening of inner wisdom, and the realization of one's true nature. It is a process of transcending the bounds of the ego and accessing higher realms of consciousness, where one experiences a revelatory sense of enmeshment, unity, and inner peace.

Theurgical techniques for spiritual illumination and enlightenment involve:

Meditation and Contemplation

Meditation and contemplative practices form the foundation for spiritual illumination and enlightenment. By stilling the mind, individuals can quiet the chatter of thoughts and connect with the deeper aspects of their being. Through regular *meditation* practice, one can encourage inner peace, clarity, and insight, leading to spiritual awakening.

Self-Inquiry and Reflection

Self-inquiry involves exploring the nature of one's self and the true nature of reality. By asking revelatory questions like "Who am I?" and investigating the nature of thoughts, emotions, and perceptions, individuals can penetrate beyond surface-level identities and gain insights into their true essence.

Study of Sacred Texts and Teachings

Engaging in the study of sacred texts, spiritual literature, and teachings can provide guidance and inspiration on the path to spiritual illumination. Diving into the wisdom and insights of enlightened masters and sacred traditions deepens understanding and supports the process of spiritual awakening.

Cultivation of Virtues

Virtues like compassion, love, humility, and non-attachment are integral to the path of spiritual illumination and enlightenment. By embodying these qualities, individuals align themselves with higher principles and open themselves to the transformative power of divine grace.

Surrender and Letting Go

Surrendering to the divine and letting go of attachments, desires, and egoic identifications is a key aspect of spiritual illumination. By releasing resistance and surrendering to the present moment, individuals open themselves to the flow of divine grace and wisdom.

Devotion and Bhakti

Devotional practices, like chanting, singing, and expressing gratitude to the divine, can encourage a deep sense of connection and devotion. By surrendering the egoic self to the divine and merging one's consciousness with the *divine presence*, individuals can experience revelatory spiritual illumination.

Connection with Nature

Connecting with the natural world and appreciating its beauty and wisdom can be a powerful catalyst for spiritual illumination. Nature acts as a mirror, reflecting the harmony and enmeshment of all, reminding individuals of their own innate divinity.

Guidance from Spiritual Teachers

Seeking guidance from enlightened teachers or spiritual mentors who have attained spiritual illumination can provide invaluable support on the path. These teachers can offer guidance, transmit teachings, and provide a direct transmission of spiritual energy that facilitates the awakening process.

Rituals and Ceremonies

Rituals and ceremonies play a significant place in *theurgy* and can serve as transformative vehicles for spiritual illumination and enlightenment. Through carefully designed rituals, individuals can create a sacred space, invoke *divine presence*, and access higher states of consciousness.

Integration of Spiritual Insights

Spiritual illumination and enlightenment are not limited to transcendent experiences but also involve the integration of insights into everyday life. It requires bringing spiritual wisdom into practical *action*, living with authenticity, and embodying the principles of love, compassion, and service.

Theurgical techniques aim to encourage spiritual illumination and enlightenment by providing individuals with practical tools to access higher states of consciousness, dissolve egoic identifications, and awaken to the truth of their being. These techniques are not meant to be separate from daily life but are intended to integrate spiritual insights into all aspects of one's existence.

It is important to note that spiritual illumination and enlightenment are not necessarily attained through a linear process or specific set of techniques. Each individual's quest is unique, and the path to spiritual awakening can unfold in different ways. *Theurgy* offers a diverse range of practices to cater to individual needs and preferences.

Ultimately, the goal of spiritual illumination and enlightenment is the direct experience of one's true nature, the recognition of the interconnection of all beings, and the embodiment of love, wisdom, and compassion. It is a revelatory awakening to the *divine essence* within and a realization of the inherent unity that underlies all existence.

In culmination, *theurgy* includes a variety of techniques for spiritual illumination and enlightenment. These techniques include *meditation*, self-inquiry, study of sacred texts, cultivation of virtues, surrender, devotion, connection with nature, guidance from spiritual teachers, rituals, and integration of spiritual insights. By engaging in these practices, individuals can awaken to higher states of consciousness, dissolve egoic identifications, and embody the wisdom, love, and compassion inherent in their true nature. The path of spiritual illumination and enlightenment is a transformative quest that leads to a revelatory realization of enmeshment and inner peace.

XXXVII: DIVINE TRANSCENDENCE AND IMMANENCE

Theurgy and the concept of *divine transcendence and immanence* are fundamental to mystical and spiritual traditions. In Greek, the term for *transcendence* is "υπεροχή" (yperochí) and the term for immanence is "ενοχή" (enochí).

Divine *transcendence* refers to the understanding that the divine exists beyond and surpasses the bounds of the material world and human comprehension. It is the recognition that the divine is beyond the scope of ordinary human experience and exists in a world that goes beyond time, space, and the physical world.

Divine immanence, on the other hand, highlights the belief that the divine is present and active within the created world. It recognizes that the divine is not distant or detached but permeates every aspect of existence, including the natural world, human beings, and the depths of consciousness.

The concept of *divine transcendence and immanence* in *theurgy* acknowledges that the divine is simultaneously beyond and within all things. It holds that the divine goes beyond human bounds and yet is intimately present in every aspect of creation.

Theurgy-breathed teachings emphasize the importance of recognizing and honoring both aspects of divine existence, understanding that they are not mutually exclusive but rather complementary. The concept of *divine transcendence and immanence* includes several key aspects:

Transcendence

Divine *transcendence* acknowledges that the divine is beyond the bounds of the physical world and human comprehension. It recognizes that the divine is infinitely huge, boundless, and incomprehensible. Divine *transcendence* highlights the awe-triggering and mysterious nature of the divine.

Immanence

Divine immanence highlights the belief that the divine is present and active within all aspects of creation. It highlights that the divine is not separate from the world but intimately involved in its unfolding. Divine immanence reflects the belief in the sacredness of all and the inherent divinity within each being.

Unity in Diversity

The concept of *divine transcendence and immanence* recognizes that although the divine is transcendent, it is also immanent in all aspects of existence. It highlights the underlying unity that connects all beings and the relationship of diversity within that unity. This understanding nurtures a sense of enmeshment and reverence for the sacredness of all life.

Mystery and Paradox

Divine transcendence and immanence contain an inherent mystery and paradox that challenges human understanding. The recognition that the divine is both beyond and within all things invites individuals to look favorably towards the limits of human comprehension and to approach the divine with humility and reverence.

Personal and Transpersonal Experience

The concept of *divine transcendence and imma-nence* acknowledges that individuals can experience the divine in both personal and transpersonal ways. Personal experiences of the divine involve direct encounters with the transcendent and immanent aspects of the divine, while transpersonal experiences involve a sense of merging with the divine or the dissolution of individual bounds.

Pathways to Union

Divine transcendence and immanence provide different pathways to seek union with the divine. Some individuals may be drawn to practices that emphasize the *transcendence* of the divine, like *contemplation, meditation,* and seeking the ineffable. Others may focus on practices that highlight the immanence of the divine, like service, devotion, and connecting with the divine in everyday life.

Balance and Harmony

The concept of *divine transcendence and immanence* calls for a balance and harmony between the recognition of the divine as transcendent and immanent. It encourages individuals to look favorably towards both aspects, recognizing that they are interconnected and mutually enriching. By balancing the awareness of *divine transcendence and immanence*, individuals can develop a holistic understanding of the divine and encourage a deeper connection with the sacred.

Theurgical practices aim to facilitate the experience and realization of *divine transcendence and immanence* through various means:

Contemplative Practices

Contemplative practices, like *meditation*, prayer, and silent reflection, provide a space for individuals to go beyond the bounds of the ordinary mind and open themselves to the transcendent aspect of the divine. Through these practices, individuals can encourage a direct experience of the divine beyond conceptual understanding.

Devotional Practices

Devotional practices, including chanting, singing, and rituals, help individuals connect with the immanent aspect of the divine. By engaging in acts of devotion and expressing reverence and gratitude, individuals can experience a sense of intimacy and connection with the *divine presence*.

Nature Connection

Connecting with nature and immersing oneself in the beauty and wisdom of the natural world can be a powerful way to experience both the *transcendence* and immanence of the divine. By observing the complex patterns of nature and recognizing the presence of the divine in every living being, individuals can deepen their understanding of *divine transcendence and immanence*.

Mystical Union

Theurgy recognizes that through mystical practices and spiritual transformation, individuals can experience a sense of union with the divine. In these revelatory moments of unity, the distinction between the transcendent and immanent aspects of the divine may dissolve, and individuals may experience the divine in a state of oneness.

Sacred Rituals

Rituals within *theurgy* create a sacred space where individuals can connect with the transcendent and immanent aspects of the divine. Through carefully designed rituals, individuals can invoke the presence of the divine, align themselves with *divine energies*, and experience a revelatory sense of connection and reverence.

Integration and Embodiment

The practice of *divine transcendence and immanence* is not limited to specific practices or experiences but extends to the integration and embodiment of this understanding in everyday life. It involves recognizing the divine in all aspects of existence and expressing the qualities of the divine in one's thoughts, words, and actions.

In culmination, the concept of *divine transcendence and immanence* in *theurgy* acknowledges that the divine is both beyond and within all things. It recognizes the awe-triggering and mysterious nature of the transcendent aspect of the divine, while emphasizing the presence and sacredness of the immanent aspect. *Theurgy*-breathed practices aim to facilitate the experience and realization of *divine transcendence and immanence* through contemplative practices, devotional practices, connection with nature, mystical union, sacred rituals, and the integration of this understanding in everyday life.

XXXVIII: EVIL AND THE DEMONIC

The place of *theurgy* in Neoplatonic theories of evil and the demonic is an intriguing aspect of these philosophical and mystical traditions. While there may not be specific Greek terms for evil and the demonic within the context of *theurgy*, Neoplatonic thought offers insights into the nature of evil and the means by which *theurgy* can address and overcome its influence.

In Neoplatonic philosophy, evil is often seen as a privation or absence of the Good rather than a positive entity in itself. The Greek term for evil, in general, is "κακό" (kakó), which refers to moral evil or something harmful or undesirable. The term for the demonic in Greek is "δαιμόνιον" (daimónion), which can refer to a supernatural being, often associated with negative or malevolent influences.

Within the scaffolding of Neoplatonic thought, *theurgy* holds a significant place in addressing the presence of evil and the demonic by seeking union with the divine and aligning oneself with the Good. *Theurgy* has designs on purifying and elevating the soul, transforming it from a state of ignorance and separation to one of knowledge and unity with the divine. Through the practice of *theurgy*, individuals can overcome the influence of evil and the demonic and restore harmony within themselves and the world.

The Neoplatonic understanding of evil and the demonic can be summarized in the following key points:

The Hierarchy of Being

Neoplatonic thought posits a hierarchical structure of existence, with the divine at the highest level and varying degrees of lesser beings below. Evil and the demonic are seen as lower manifestations in this hierarchy, resulting from the separation from the divine and a distortion of the Good.

The Place of Ignorance

Ignorance is determined a fundamental aspect of evil. The Neoplatonists believed that the soul's ignorance and forgetfulness of its *divine origin* and true nature led to a state of separation and the potential for evil actions. *Theurgy* has designs on restoring knowledge and awareness of the divine, thus overcoming ignorance and its consequences.

The Principle of Ascent

Neoplatonic philosophy highlights the *soul's quest* of ascent back to its *divine source*. Evil and the demonic are viewed as obstacles along this path, arising from attachments to the material world and the lower aspects of existence. *Theurgy* provides techniques and practices to aid in this ascent, purifying the soul and aligning it with the divine.

The Purification of the Soul

Theurgy recognizes the importance of purifying the soul as a means of overcoming the influence of evil and the demonic. This *purification* process involves the elimination of negative influences, vices, and attachments that hinder the soul's union with the divine. *Theurgy* employs rituals, prayers, *contemplation*, and other practices to facilitate this *purification*.

The Power of Divine Grace

Divine grace is seen as an essential force in combating evil and the demonic. The Neoplatonists believed that through *theurgy*, individuals could attract and receive divine grace, which empowers and guides them on their spiritual quest. Divine grace helps to counteract the negative influences and supports the soul in its quest for union with the divine.

The Transformation of Evil

Theurgy seeks to transform evil rather than eradicate it completely. It recognizes that evil and the demonic serve a purpose in the larger cosmic order, allowing for the exercise of free will and the opportunity for growth and spiritual development. Through the transformative power of *theurgy*, evil can be transmuted into a means for the soul's *purification* and eventual reunion with the divine.

The Unity of All Beings

Neoplatonic thought highlights the unity of all beings and the enmeshment of existence. Evil and the demonic are understood as distortions and deviations from this underlying unity. *Theurgy* pursues the restoration of this unity by aligning the individual soul with the divine, thereby contributing to the restoration of harmony and the diminishment of evil's influence.

In practical terms, *theurgy* offers a variety of techniques and practices to combat evil and the demonic:

Rituals of Purification

Theurgy employs rituals designed to purify the soul and cleanse it from negative influences. These rituals may involve the use of sacred *symbols*, invocations, offerings, and the recitation of prayers or hymns.

Invocation of Divine Names and Powers

Theurgy harnesses the power of *divine names and attributes* in its practices. Through the *invocation* of specific divine names and the recognition of their qualities, the practitioner seeks to align with the divine and draw upon its transformative and protective energies.

Contemplative Practices

Contemplative practices like *meditation*, reflection, and *contemplation* of divine truths are employed in *theurgy* to encourage spiritual awareness and insight. These practices help individuals to discern the true nature of evil, its causes, and the means to go beyond its influence.

Devotional Practices

Devotion to the divine, expressed through acts of reverence, gratitude, and surrender, is a central component of *theurgy*. Devotional practices help to strengthen the connection with the divine, invoking its grace and protection in the face of evil.

Knowledge and Wisdom

Theurgy recognizes the importance of knowledge and wisdom in overcoming evil. Through the study of sacred texts, philosophical teachings, and spiritual insights, individuals gain the understanding and discernment necessary to navigate the spiritual path and counteract the influences of evil and the demonic.

Ethical Conduct

Theurgy highlights the importance of ethical conduct and virtuous living. By cultivating virtues like compassion, love, humility, and integrity, individuals align themselves with the divine and minimize the potential for evil actions.

It is important to note that the Neoplatonic approach to evil and the demonic within the context of *theurgy* is highly nuanced and complex. The understanding and techniques employed may vary among different Neoplatonic philosophers and schools of thought.

In culmination, *theurgy* holds a significant place in addressing the presence of evil and the demonic within Neoplatonic philosophy. By seeking union with the divine and aligning oneself with the Good, *theurgy* offers a means to overcome the influence of evil. Through the *purification* of the soul, the cultivation of divine grace, and the transformation of evil, individuals can restore harmony within themselves and the world.

Theurgy employs rituals, *invocation* of divine names, contemplative practices, devotional acts, the pursuit of knowledge and wisdom, and ethical conduct to combat evil and the demonic and facilitate the soul's ascent to union with the divine.

XXXIX: DIVINE BEAUTY

Theurgy and the concept of *divine beauty* are intertwined in the mystical and philosophical traditions that explore the nature of the divine and its manifestation in the world. While there isn't a specific Greek term for *divine beauty* within the context of *theurgy*, the Greek term for beauty is "κάλλος" (kállos), which refers to both physical and spiritual beauty, as well as harmony, excellence, and aesthetic perfection.

In the practice of *theurgy*, *divine beauty* includes both the inherent beauty of the divine itself and the recognition of beauty as a transformative force that leads individuals closer to the divine. It is the expression of *divine qualities* and attributes that evoke a sense of awe, wonder, and reverence in those who perceive it.

Here are some key aspects and insights into the place of *theurgy* in understanding and experiencing *divine beauty*:

Perceiving the Divine Beauty

Theurgy invites individuals to develop an awareness and sensitivity to the beauty that permeates the cosmos. It encourages the cultivation of a receptive and contemplative state of mind that allows one to perceive the *divine beauty* in all things, both seen and unseen.

Transcendent and Immanent Beauty

Divine beauty is understood to exist both in its transcendent form, beyond the bounds of the material world, and in its immanent form, manifested within creation. *Theurgy* acknowledges that the beauty of the divine is present in all aspects of existence, starting with the grandeur of nature to the subtleties of human experience.

Harmony and Proportion

Divine beauty is often associated with harmony and proportion. *Theurgy* recognizes that the divine is the source of cosmic order and balance. It teaches that when individuals align themselves with the divine, they become channels for this harmony and embody the principles of beauty in their thoughts, actions, and creations.

Aesthetic Experience

Theurgy highlights the place of aesthetic experience in perceiving *divine beauty*. Aesthetic experiences, like encountering *art, music, poetry,* and nature, can evoke a sense of awe and transport individuals to a higher state of consciousness. *Theurgy* recognizes these experiences as gateways to the divine and utilizes them to facilitate spiritual transformation.

Transformation through Beauty

The recognition and appreciation of *divine beauty* have the power to transform individuals at a deep level. Beauty acts as a catalyst for inner awakening, triggering individuals to seek higher truths, encourage virtues, and align their lives with the divine. Through *theurgy*, individuals can actively engage with beauty as a transformative force.

Divine Archetypes

Theurgy acknowledges the existence of archetypal forms or ideals of beauty that are expressions of the divine. These archetypal forms serve as inspiration for human creativity, reflecting the underlying patterns and principles of *divine beauty*. *Theurgy* provides practices and rituals to connect with these archetypal forms and to channel their transformative power.

Transcending Material Beauty

While *theurgy* recognizes the beauty present in the material world, it also acknowledges that material beauty is only a reflection of a higher, transcendent beauty. The ultimate aim is to move beyond the superficial allure of material beauty and to seek a direct encounter with the source of all beauty—the divine itself.

Beauty as a Path to Union

Theurgy teaches that beauty can be a path to union with the divine. The experience of beauty opens individuals to a heightened state of consciousness and transports them beyond the bounds of the egoic self. In this state, individuals can experience a sense of oneness with the divine and a deep connection to the underlying beauty of all creation.

Creative Expression

Theurgy recognizes the power of creative expression as a means to embody and reflect *divine beauty*. Through *art, music, poetry*, and other creative endeavors, individuals can channel the *divine qualities* of beauty and inspirit others to perceive the transcendent dimensions of reality.

Beauty as an Essential Attribute of the Divine

In *theurgy*, beauty is determined an essential attribute of the divine. It is inseparable from the divine nature and is viewed as one of the ways in which the divine reveals itself to humanity. *Theurgy* provides practices that enable individuals to attune themselves to the frequency of *divine beauty* and to participate in its manifestation.

Theurgical practices that facilitate the experience and expression of *divine beauty* include:

Contemplation and Meditation

By cultivating a state of *contemplation* and deep inner stillness, individuals can open themselves to the perception of *divine beauty*. Through *meditation*, they can attune their awareness to the subtle dimensions of existence and awaken to the beauty that underlies all things.

Rituals and Sacred Spaces

Theurgy employs rituals and the creation of sacred spaces to invoke and honor *divine beauty*. These rituals may include the use of *symbols*, sacred geometry, and the arrangement of sacred objects to create a harmonious and aesthetically pleasing environment that facilitates the connection with the divine.

Cultivation of Virtues

Theurgy recognizes that the cultivation of virtues is essential in manifesting *divine beauty* in one's life. Virtues like love, compassion, kindness, and integrity reflect the *divine qualities* of beauty and contribute to the creation of harmonious relationships and a more beautiful world.

Connection with Nature

Nature is regarded as a manifestation of *divine beauty*. *Theurgy* encourages individuals to spend time in natural environments, appreciating the beauty and wisdom inherent in the natural world. Through this connection, individuals can attune themselves to the rhythm of nature and deepen their understanding of *divine beauty*.

Expressive Arts

Theurgy embraces the expressive arts as a means to communicate and reflect *divine beauty*. Artistic practices like painting, sculpture, *music*, dance, and *poetry* allow individuals to channel their inner experiences of *divine beauty* and share them with others.

Embodying Divine Beauty

Theurgy highlights the embodiment of *divine beauty* in everyday life. This involves integrating the principles of beauty into thoughts, words, and actions. By aligning with the *divine qualities* of beauty, individuals can become vessels for the expression of *divine beauty* in the world.

In culmination, *theurgy* and the concept of *divine beauty* are closely intertwined in the mystical and philosophical traditions. *Divine beauty* is both transcendent and immanent, encompassing harmony, proportion, and aesthetic perfection. *Theurgy* provides practices and techniques to awaken individuals to the perception of *divine beauty* and to facilitate its manifestation in their lives. By attuning themselves to the frequency of *divine beauty*, individuals can experience transformation, deepen their connection with the divine, and contribute to the creation of a more beautiful and harmonious world.

XL: DIVINE INSPIRATION AND CREATIVITY

Theurgical techniques for *divine inspiration* and creativity are central to the practice of *theurgy*, which seeks to establish a connection with the divine and channel its transformative energies. While there may not be specific Greek terms for *divine inspiration* and creativity within the context of *theurgy*, the Greek term for inspiration is "εμπνεύση" (emnefsi), which signifies the infusion of divine or spiritual influence, and the term for creativity is "δημιουργικότητα" (dimiourgikóti-ta), which refers to the ability to bring something new or original into existence.

Theurgy recognizes that *divine inspiration* and creativity flow from the *divine source* and are channeled through individuals who attune themselves to its frequencies. These techniques aim to encourage a receptive state of mind, remove obstacles to creativity, and establish a direct connection with the divine for the purpose of breathed and transformative expression.

Here are some key aspects and techniques related to *divine inspiration* and creativity in *theurgy*:

Cultivating Receptivity

Theurgy highlights the cultivation of a receptive state of mind as a foundation for *divine inspiration* and creativity. This involves quieting the chatter of the ordinary mind, cultivating inner stillness, and creating space for the divine to communicate and inspirit.

Inner Silence and Contemplation

Techniques like *meditation, contemplation*, and mindfulness help individuals to encourage inner silence and clarity. By quieting the mental chatter and sharpening the attention inward, one can create an environment conducive to receiving *divine inspiration* and insights.

Invocation and Prayer

Invocation and prayer are powerful techniques employed in *theurgy* to establish a direct connection with the divine. Through the use of sacred words, prayers, and invocations, individuals call upon the *divine forces* and seek their guidance, inspiration, and creative energy.

Rituals and Sacred Space

Rituals and the creation of sacred space provide a structured scaffolding for *divine inspiration* and creativity. *Theurgy* utilizes *symbols*, sacred objects, and specific rituals to evoke a heightened state of awareness and to invite the *divine presence* to inspirit and guide the creative process.

Harmonizing with Divine Energies

Theurgy recognizes that different *divine energies* correspond to different aspects of creativity. By attuning oneself to specific *divine qualities*, like beauty, wisdom, or harmony, individuals can align their creative expression with these energies and evoke their transformative power.

Embodying Divine Archetypes

Divine archetypes serve as sources of inspiration and creative expression. *Theurgy* provides techniques to connect with and embody these archetypal energies, enabling individuals to access their transformative potential in the creative process.

Symbolic Language and Imagery

Theurgy employs symbolic language and imagery as vehicles for *divine inspiration* and creative expression. *Symbols* carry deep layers of meaning and can serve as bridges between the conscious and unconscious mind, facilitating the reception of *divine inspiration* and the communication of transformative ideas.

Flow State and Intuition

Theurgy recognizes the importance of accessing the flow state, a state of heightened concentration and absorption in an activity. When individuals are in a flow state, they are more open to intuitive insights and creative inspiration. Techniques that promote relaxation, concentration, and mindfulness can help individuals access this state and tap into their intuitive wisdom.

Integration of Mind, Heart, and Body

Theurgy highlights the integration of the mind, heart, and body in the creative process. By harmonizing these aspects of the self, individuals create a balanced and coherent vessel for *divine inspiration* to flow through. Practices like breathwork, movement, and embodiment exercises help to integrate these dimensions and enhance creative expression.

Creative Rituals and Practices

Theurgy incorporates creative rituals and practices that specifically aim to invoke *divine inspiration* and channel creative energy. These rituals may involve the use of *music*, dance, visual arts, writing, or other creative mediums as ways to engage with the divine and express one's unique creative vision.

Surrendering the Ego

Divine inspiration and creativity often flourish when the egoic self is transcended. *Theurgy* encourages individuals to let go of personal agendas, expectations, and attachments in order to allow the divine to *work* through them. By surrendering the egoic self, individuals become conduits for the expression of *divine inspiration* and creative energy.

Continuous Refinement and Growth

Theurgical techniques for *divine inspiration* and creativity are not fixed or static. They evolve and deepen through continuous practice, refinement, and self-exploration. *Theurgy* encourages individuals to remain open to new insights, to look favorably towards experimentation, and to encourage a lifelong commitment to personal and creative growth.

By employing these techniques, individuals engage in a co-creative process with the divine, accessing a revelatory source of inspiration and expressing it in transformative and creative ways. *Theurgy* recognizes that *divine inspiration* and creativity have the potential to bring forth new insights, beauty, and meaningful contributions to both the individual and the collective.

In culmination, *theurgy* offers a valuable array of techniques for individuals to connect with *divine in-*

spiration and creativity. By cultivating receptivity, establishing a direct connection with the divine, and aligning with its transformative energies, individuals can tap into a wellspring of inspiration and bring forth creative expressions that are infused with the qualities of the divine. Through practices like *meditation*, prayer, rituals, harmonization with *divine energies*, symbolic language, and surrendering the ego, *theurgy* facilitates the co-creative partnership between individuals and the divine, allowing for breathed and transformative acts of creation.

XLI: DIVINE TRUTH

Theurgy and the concept of *divine truth* are closely connected in the philosophical and mystical traditions that explore the nature of ultimate reality and the means by which individuals can attain knowledge of that reality. While there may not be a specific Greek term for *divine truth* within the context of *theurgy*, the Greek term for truth is "αλήθεια" (alétheia), which signifies the state or quality of being true or in accordance with reality.

Within the practice of *theurgy*, *divine truth* refers to a deeper understanding of reality and the divine. It includes the recognition of the ultimate truth that underlies all existence, as well as the means by which individuals can attain knowledge of that truth.

Here are some key aspects and insights into the place of *theurgy* in understanding and experiencing *divine truth*:

Seeking the Ultimate Truth

Theurgy recognizes the inherent human quest for truth and the desire to understand reality. It acknowledges that the ultimate truth goes beyond the bounds of ordinary perception and is to be found through direct experiential knowledge.

The Divine as the Source of Truth

Theurgy posits that the divine is the ultimate source of truth. It is from the divine that all truths emanate and to which they ultimately lead. *Theurgy* offers techniques and practices to establish a connection with the divine and to attain insights into the ultimate truth.

Inner Transformation for Truth Attainment

Theurgy highlights that the attainment of *divine truth* requires an inner transformation of the individual. It involves purifying the mind, transcending the bounds of the egoic self, and aligning one's consciousness with the divine. Through this transformation, individuals gain access to higher levels of truth and understanding.

Direct Experience of Truth

Theurgy places great emphasis on the direct experiential knowledge of truth. It encourages individuals to go beyond mere intellectual understanding and to seek direct communion with the divine. Through *contemplation, meditation,* and other practices, individuals can have direct experiences that reveal truths that surpass ordinary conceptual understanding.

Transcending Relative Truths

Theurgy acknowledges that there are different levels of truth, including relative or conventional truths that are valid within specific contexts. However, it also highlights the need to go beyond these relative truths and to uncover the deeper, absolute truths that are universal and timeless.

Unity of Truth

Theurgy recognizes the unity and enmeshment of all truths. It teaches that the different domains of knowledge, like philosophy, science, spirituality, and mysticism, are ultimately seeking to understand different aspects of the same underlying truth. *Theurgy's* goal is to integrate these different perspectives and to reveal the harmony and coherence of the ultimate truth.

Discernment and Discrimination

Theurgy highlights the importance of discernment and discrimination in the pursuit of truth. It recognizes that not all beliefs, teachings, or experiences are aligned with the ultimate truth. *Theurgy* provides practices and techniques to develop discernment and to distinguish between true insights and distortions.

Alignment with Divine Wisdom

Theurgy teaches that *divine wisdom* is a key aspect of *divine truth*. Wisdom involves not just knowledge but also understanding and the proper application of knowledge in a way that aligns with the divine. *Theurgy* seeks to encourage wisdom through the alignment with *divine qualities* and the integration of spiritual insights into one's life.

Harmonizing Intellect and Intuition

Theurgy recognizes the value of both intellect and intuition in the pursuit of truth. It encourages individuals to encourage intellectual rigor and critical thinking, while also honoring the intuitive faculties that can directly perceive truth beyond the bounds of rationality. *Theurgy* provides practices that harmonize these faculties and facilitate the integration of intellectual and intuitive insights.

The Transformative Power of Truth

Theurgy acknowledges that *divine truth* has a transformative power. When individuals align themselves with the truth and integrate it into their lives, they experience a revelatory shift in consciousness and a deepening of their connection with the divine. Truth acts as a catalyst for personal growth, spiritual development, and the realization of one's highest potential.

Theurgical practices that facilitate the attainment of *divine truth* include:

Contemplation and Meditation

Theurgy employs contemplative practices to quiet the mind, focus awareness, and deepen understanding. Through *contemplation* and *meditation*, individuals can develop insights into reality and attain direct experiences of truth.

Sacred Study and Reflection

Theurgy encourages the study of sacred texts, philosophical writings, and spiritual teachings as a means to deepen understanding and engage in intellectual inquiry. Reflection on these teachings helps individuals assimilate and integrate the truths they contain.

Rituals and Sacraments

Rituals and sacraments in *theurgy* serve as means of connecting with the divine and accessing deeper levels of truth. These practices create sacred spaces and invoke the presence of the divine, facilitating transformative experiences and insights.

Communion with Divine Beings

Theurgy acknowledges that *divine beings* can serve as guides and sources of truth. Through prayer, invocations, and rituals, individuals can establish communion with these beings, receiving their guidance and insights.

Inquiry and Questioning

Theurgy encourages individuals to inquire deeply into reality and to question assumptions and beliefs. By engaging in a process of self-inquiry and critical examination, individuals can uncover hidden truths and go beyond limited perspectives.

Integration of Intuitive Insights

Theurgy recognizes the importance of intuitive insights in the pursuit of truth. It provides techniques to enhance intuition and to integrate intuitive insights into one's understanding and actions.

Living in Alignment with Truth

Theurgy highlights that living in alignment with truth is essential for the realization of *divine truth*. It encourages individuals to embody and express the truths they have attained through their thoughts, words, and actions.

In culmination, *theurgy* offers a pathway to attaining and experiencing *divine truth*. By establishing a connection with the divine, engaging in practices that encourage inner transformation, and seeking direct experiences of truth, individuals can deepen their understanding of the ultimate nature of reality. *Theurgy* recognizes that *divine truth* goes beyond conventional knowledge and is accessed through direct experiential insight. Through the cultivation of discernment, the harmonization of intellect and intuition, and the integration of *divine wisdom*, individuals can align themselves with the transformative power of truth and embody it in their lives.

XLII: Divine Harmony

Theurgy and the concept of *divine harmony* are intricately connected in the mystical and philosophical traditions that seek to understand the nature of the divine and its manifestation in the world. While there may not be a specific Greek term for *divine harmony* within the context of *theurgy*, the Greek term for harmony is "αρμονία" (armonía), which signifies a state of balance, order, and coherence.

Divine harmony in *theurgy* includes both the inherent harmony of the divine itself and the recognition of harmony as a fundamental principle that permeates all aspects of existence. It is the expression of balance, coherence, and enmeshment that brings about a sense of unity and beauty in the cosmos.

Here are some key aspects and insights into the place of *theurgy* in understanding and experiencing *divine harmony*:

Harmonizing with the Divine

Theurgy teaches that individuals can harmonize their thoughts, emotions, and actions with the divine in order to align themselves with the inherent harmony of the cosmos. By attuning themselves to the *divine qualities* and principles of harmony, individuals can encourage a sense of balance and coherence within themselves and in their relationship with the world.

Balance and Equilibrium

Divine harmony involves the maintenance of balance and equilibrium between different aspects of existence. This includes the balance between the spiritual and the material, the rational and the intuitive, the masculine and the feminine, and the individual and the collective. *Theurgy* recognizes the importance of cultivating and preserving these harmonious relationships.

Unity and Enmeshment

Divine harmony acknowledges the enmeshment of all. It recognizes that everything in the cosmos is interlaced in a nexus of relationships and that each individual part contributes to the overall harmony of the whole. *Theurgy* provides practices and teachings to deepen individuals' awareness of this enmeshment and to encourage a sense of unity with all beings.

Cosmic Order

Theurgy acknowledges that the divine is the source of cosmic order. The *divine qualities* of wisdom, intelligence, and creative power establish a harmonious scaffolding within which the cosmos operates. *Theurgy* searches out the underlying principles and patterns of this cosmic order and offers techniques to align oneself with them.

Harmony in Nature

Theurgy recognizes the inherent harmony in the natural world. The cycles of seasons, the symphony of sounds in the natural environment, and the enmeshment of ecosystems all reflect the *divine harmony* that underlies creation. *Theurgy* encourages individuals to connect with nature and to appreciate and learn from its harmonious rhythms.

Inner Harmony

Theurgy highlights the cultivation of inner harmony as a prerequisite for experiencing and expressing *divine harmony*. This involves harmonizing the different aspects of the self—body, mind, emotions, and spirit—and creating an inner coherence that allows individuals to be in alignment with the *divine qualities* of harmony.

Harmonizing the Ego

Theurgy recognizes that the egoic self can create disharmony and discord. It teaches that by transcending the ego and its attachments, individuals can align themselves with the *divine will* and participate in the greater harmony of the cosmos. *Theurgy* provides techniques to *work* with the ego and to encourage humility, surrender, and selflessness.

Harmonious Relationships

Divine harmony extends to interpersonal relationships and social dynamics. *Theurgy* highlights the cultivation of virtues like compassion, empathy, and cooperation, which encourage harmonious interactions and contribute to the collective harmony of communities and societies.

Beauty and Aesthetics

Divine harmony is closely associated with beauty and aesthetics. *Theurgy* recognizes that beauty is an expression of harmony and that aesthetic experiences can evoke a sense of awe and wonder, leading individuals closer to the divine. *Theurgy* incorporates artistic practices, rituals, and the appreciation of beauty as means to connect with *divine harmony*.

Integration of Polarities

Theurgy acknowledges the existence of polarities and dualities in the world and teaches the integration of these opposing forces to achieve harmony. This includes the integration of light and dark, masculine and feminine, and positive and negative aspects of existence. By reconciling these polarities within oneself, individuals can contribute to the greater harmony of the cosmos.

Theurgical practices that facilitate the experience and expression of *divine harmony* include:

Meditation and Contemplation

Theurgy employs *meditation* and contemplative practices to encourage inner stillness, clarity, and harmony. Through these practices, individuals can attune themselves to the frequencies of *divine harmony* and experience a sense of unity and coherence.

Rituals and Ceremonies

Rituals and ceremonies in *theurgy* serve as means of invoking and honoring the *divine qualities* of harmony. These rituals may include the use of sacred *symbols, music,* dance, and other aesthetic elements that create a harmonious and sacred atmosphere.

Breathwork and Energy Practices

Theurgy recognizes the necessary place of energy in maintaining harmony within the body and the subtle energy system. Techniques like breathwork, pranayama, and energy practices help individuals balance and harmonize their energy, promoting overall wellness and alignment with the divine.

Sacred Geometry and Proportions

Theurgy searches out the principles of sacred geometry and proportions, which are believed to reflect the underlying harmony of the cosmos. By working with sacred geometric patterns and ratios, individuals can align themselves with the harmonious principles that govern the universe.

Integration of Divine Qualities

Theurgy invites individuals to encourage and embody the *divine qualities* of harmony in their thoughts, emotions, and actions. By consciously integrating these qualities into their daily lives, individuals contribute to the overall harmony of the world.

Harmonious Communication

Theurgy highlights the importance of harmonious communication and speech. It encourages individuals to speak truthfully, kindly, and with respect for others, encouraging harmonious relationships and contributing to a more harmonious social environment.

Harmonizing with Nature

Theurgy encourages individuals to spend time in nature, observing and connecting with its harmonious rhythms. By attuning oneself to the natural world, individuals can learn from its wisdom and integrate its harmonious qualities into their own lives.

Harmonious Creativity

Theurgy recognizes the power of creative expression as a means to embody and reflect *divine harmony*. Through artistic practices like *music*, dance, painting, and writing, individuals can channel the harmonious energies of the divine and inspirit others to experience and look favorably towards harmony.

In culmination, *theurgy* offers a pathway to experiencing and expressing *divine harmony*. By aligning oneself with the inherent harmony of the divine, cultivating inner harmony, harmonizing relationships, and appreciating the harmony in nature, individuals can participate in the greater harmony of the cosmos. *Theurgy* recognizes that *divine harmony* is a unifying principle that brings coherence, beauty, and balance to all aspects of existence. Through practices that encourage awareness, balance, and integration, individuals can attune themselves to the frequencies of *divine harmony* and contribute to the creation of a more harmonious and unified world.

XLIII: Neoplatonic Theories of Language and Communication

Theurgy holds a significant place in Neoplatonic theories of language and communication, offering insights into the nature of language, its relationship to the divine, and its potential for conveying revelatory truths. While there may not be a specific Greek term for the place of *theurgy* in Neoplatonic theories of language and communication, we can explore the Greek term "λόγος" (logos), which refers to the divine principle of reason, order, and communication.

In Neoplatonic thought, language is seen as a powerful tool for expressing and conveying knowledge, but it is also recognized as limited and prone to distortion. *Theurgy* provides a scaffolding for understanding the transformative potential of language and offers techniques to refine and elevate its use in order to align it with *divine truth*.

Here are some key aspects and insights into the place of *theurgy* in Neoplatonic theories of language and communication:

Divine Logos

Neoplatonic philosophy recognizes the existence of a divine Logos, an emanation of the divine that acts as the source of all existence and the underlying principle of order and reason. This divine Logos is the foundation of all meaningful communication and provides the template for the harmonious expression of language.

Language as a Reflective Medium

Theurgy acknowledges that language, in its ordinary usage, often falls short of capturing the full depth and complexity of divine truths. It is seen as a reflective medium that attempts to convey and represent higher realities, but it is limited by the imperfections of human expression and comprehension.

Symbolic Language

Theurgy recognizes the power of *symbols* in communicating revelatory truths. *Symbols* are determined vehicles for transcending the bounds of ordinary language and conveying deeper meanings that vibe with the divine. *Symbols* enable individuals to access higher levels of understanding and to connect with the archetypal realms.

Divine Inspiration and Revelation

Theurgy highlights the importance of *divine inspiration* and revelation in the process of language and communication. Through practices like *meditation*, prayer, and *ritual*, individuals can open themselves to the influx of *divine inspiration*, which can infuse their words and expressions with greater depth and clarity.

Purification of Language

Theurgy highlights the need for the *purification* of language as a means to align it with *divine truth*. This involves cultivating clarity, precision, and integrity in one's use of language, as well as purifying one's intentions and motives in communication. By purifying language, individuals can create a more transparent and authentic channel for the expression of divine truths.

Harmonization of Language and Thought

Theurgy recognizes the enmeshment of language and thought. It teaches that by cultivating clarity and coherence in one's thinking, individuals can improve their ability to communicate effectively and accurately convey their insights and experiences. Through practices like *contemplation* and *meditation*, individuals can harmonize their language with the deeper truths they have realized.

Invocation and Affirmation

Theurgy employs techniques of *invocation* and affirmation to harness the power of language for transformative purposes. By consciously invoking *divine qualities* and affirming divine truths, individuals can align themselves with the divine Logos and use language as a means to access higher levels of understanding and to bring about positive change.

Metaphysics of Language

Neoplatonic theories of language explore the metaphysical dimensions of communication. They dive into questions about the relationship between language and reality, the place of language in shaping our perception of the world, and the ways in which language can participate in the manifestation of divine truths.

Unity of Language and Thought

Theurgy recognizes that language and thought are intertwined and that they influence and shape each other. It highlights the importance of cultivating clarity, coherence, and harmony in both language and thought, as they are mutually reinforcing. By aligning language and thought with divine truths, individuals can deepen their understanding and contribute to the manifestation of *divine order* in the world.

The Power of Naming

Theurgy acknowledges the power of naming and the importance of divine names in the process of communication. Names are seen as vehicles for invoking and evoking specific qualities and energies associated with the divine. By using names consciously and respectfully, individuals can tap into the transformative power inherent in language.

Communication with the Divine

Theurgy recognizes that language and communication can extend beyond the world of human interaction to include communication with the divine. Through prayer, *invocation*, and other spiritual practices, individuals can establish a direct connection with the divine and engage in a form of communication that goes beyond ordinary language.

Silence and Non-Verbal Communication

Theurgy acknowledges the bounds of language and the importance of silence and non-verbal communication in the world of divine communication. Silence is seen as a space for deeper communion with the divine, beyond the confines of language. Non-verbal forms of expression, like *music*, *art*, and dance, are also recognized as powerful means of communicating and evoking divine truths.

Theurgical practices that facilitate the refinement and elevation of language and communication include:

Contemplation and Meditation

Theurgy employs contemplative practices to encourage clarity, coherence, and depth in one's thinking and expression. Through *contemplation* and *meditation*, individuals can refine their use of language and align it with higher truths.

Sacred Study

Theurgy encourages the study of sacred texts, philosophical writings, and spiritual teachings as a means to deepen understanding and refine one's use of language. Sacred study provides a valuable source of inspiration and insights for the expression of divine truths.

Rituals and Invocations

Rituals and invocations in *theurgy* serve as means to invoke and honor the *divine qualities* and to align oneself with the divine Logos. These practices provide a scaffolding for conscious and intentional use of language in communication with the divine.

Symbolic Language and Imagery

Theurgy recognizes the power of symbolic language and imagery in conveying deeper truths. By working with *symbols*, individuals can communicate revelatory insights that surpass the bounds of ordinary language and engage with the archetypal realms.

Ethical Communication

Theurgy highlights the importance of ethical communication, which includes honesty, respect, and compassion. Ethical communication creates a harmonious and supportive environment for the expression of divine truths and nurtures deeper connections between individuals.

Devotional Practices

Devotional practices in *theurgy*, like prayer and chanting, provide opportunities for individuals to express their devotion and gratitude to the divine through language. These practices encourage a heart-centered approach to communication and encourage a deepening relationship with the divine.

Transcendent Silence

Theurgy recognizes the transformative power of silence and the importance of embracing moments of non-verbal communication. Silence allows for communion with the divine beyond the bounds of language and provides space for intuitive insights and direct experiences of truth.

In culmination, *theurgy* offers revelatory insights into the place of language and communication in the context of divine truths. It recognizes the bounds of ordinary language, the power of *symbols*, and the transformative potential of refined and elevated communication that aligns with the divine Logos. Through practices of *purification, invocation,* and alignment with *divine qualities,* individuals can refine their use of language and tap into the transformative power of communication. *Theurgy* acknowledges the enmeshment of language, thought, and reality, and searches out the metaphysical dimensions of communication. By harmonizing language and thought, invoking *divine qualities*, and cultivating ethical and heart-centered communication, individuals can deepen their understanding of divine truths and participate in the manifestation of *divine order* in the world.

XLIV: DIVINE KNOWLEDGE

Theurgy is intimately connected to the concept of *divine knowledge* in various mystical and philosophical traditions. While there may not be a specific Greek term for the place of *theurgy* in relation to *divine knowledge,* the Greek term "γνῶσις" (gnosis) includes the concept of deep spiritual knowledge and understanding.

Theurgy recognizes that *divine knowledge* is not limited to intellectual or rational understanding but involves a direct and experiential connection with the divine. It includes insights, wisdom, and truths that surpass ordinary human knowledge and are revealed through spiritual practices and divine revelation. Here are some key aspects and insights into the place of *theurgy* in relation to *divine knowledge*:

Direct Revelation

Theurgy acknowledges that *divine knowledge* can be directly revealed to individuals through spiritual experiences, visions, and mystical encounters. It recognizes that there is a level of knowledge that goes beyond what can be obtained through ordinary means of learning and reasoning.

Intuitive Knowing

Divine knowledge often goes beyond the bounds of linear thinking and rationality. *Theurgy* recognizes the importance of intuitive knowing, which involves a direct apprehension of truth that bypasses the intellect. Intuition allows individuals to tap into deeper levels of understanding and access higher realms of knowledge.

Spiritual Practices

Theurgy provides a scaffolding of spiritual practices that facilitate the attainment of *divine knowledge*. These practices may include *meditation, contemplation, prayer, ritual,* and *purification* techniques. By engaging in these practices, individuals can encourage a receptive state of mind and open themselves to the inflow of *divine knowledge*.

Union with the Divine

Theurgy teaches that union with the divine is a pathway to acquiring *divine knowledge*. Through practices like prayer, devotion, and mystical *contemplation*, individuals can merge their consciousness with the divine and gain direct access to *divine wisdom* and understanding.

Symbolic Language

Theurgy recognizes the power of *symbols* and symbolic language in conveying and transmitting *divine knowledge*. *Symbols* can serve as gateways to higher truths and can evoke revelatory insights and understanding beyond the bounds of ordinary language.

Unity of Knowledge and Being

Theurgy highlights that true knowledge is not merely intellectual but involves a transformation of one's being. It recognizes the inseparable connection between knowledge and personal transformation, where the acquisition of knowledge leads to an expansion of consciousness and a deepening of spiritual awareness.

Harmonization of Intellect and Intuition

Theurgy acknowledges the harmonization of intellect and intuition in the pursuit of *divine knowledge*. While intuitive knowing is highly valued, intellectual discernment is also important in order to interpret and integrate divine insights into the human experience. *Theurgy* seeks to balance these two aspects, recognizing the value of both reason and intuition.

The Divine as the Source of Knowledge

Theurgy recognizes that the ultimate source of all knowledge is the divine itself. The divine is seen as the wellspring of wisdom, truth, and understanding. Through *theurgical practices*, individuals can attune themselves to the *divine source* of knowledge and access a higher level of understanding.

Transformation of Consciousness

Theurgy acknowledges that the acquisition of *divine knowledge* is transformative. It involves a shift in consciousness and a deepening of spiritual awareness. *Theurgical practices* facilitate this transformation by purifying the mind, expanding the intellect, and aligning the individual with the divine principles of knowledge.

Ethical and Moral Knowledge

Theurgy recognizes that *divine knowledge* includes not just intellectual and metaphysical understanding but also ethical and moral insights. It highlights the importance of integrating spiritual knowledge into one's actions and living in alignment with divine principles of goodness, compassion, and integrity.

Divine Grace

Theurgy acknowledges the place of divine grace in the acquisition of knowledge. *Divine knowledge* is not solely dependent on human effort or intellect but is also bestowed through divine grace and revelation. Individuals are seen as recipients of divine gifts of knowledge, which are granted through a deep connection with the divine.

Transcending Dualities

Theurgy teaches that *divine knowledge* goes beyond dualities and bounds. It includes a holistic understanding that reconciles apparent opposites and integrates diverse perspectives. Through *theurgical practices*, individuals can go beyond limited perspectives and access a higher level of wisdom that embraces unity and wholeness.

Theurgical practices that facilitate the acquisition of *divine knowledge* include:

Meditation and Contemplation

Theurgy utilizes *meditation* and contemplative practices to quiet the mind, expand awareness, and open oneself to divine insights and revelations. Through these practices, individuals can encourage a receptive state of mind and create space for the influx of *divine knowledge*.

Prayer and Devotion

Theurgy encourages prayer and devotion as means of establishing a direct connection with the divine. Through prayer, individuals can express their longing for *divine knowledge* and seek guidance and illumination from the *divine source*.

Ritual and Symbolic Practices

Rituals and symbolic practices in *theurgy* serve as gateways to *divine knowledge*. These practices involve the use of symbolic language, sacred gestures, and *ritual* actions that evoke deeper meanings and insights beyond ordinary language.

Study of Sacred Texts

Theurgy recognizes the importance of studying sacred texts, philosophical writings, and spiritual teachings as a means of deepening one's understanding of *divine knowledge*. Sacred texts are seen as repositories of wisdom and insights that can illuminate the path to *divine knowledge*.

Purification and Asceticism

Theurgy highlights the *purification* of the mind, body, and spirit as a prerequisite for the acquisition of *divine knowledge*. *Purification* practices like fasting, self-discipline, and ethical conduct create a conducive inner environment for the reception of divine insights.

Cultivation of Virtues

Theurgy recognizes that the cultivation of virtues is essential for the acquisition and integration of *divine knowledge*. Virtues like humility, openness, sincerity, and compassion create a receptive and aligned state of being that allows for the influx of *divine wisdom*.

Cultivating Intuition

Theurgy encourages the cultivation of intuition as a means of accessing *divine knowledge*. Intuition is seen as a direct channel of communication with the divine and provides insights that surpass the bounds of ordinary reasoning.

Integration of Knowledge and Experience

Theurgy highlights the integration of knowledge and experience. *Divine knowledge* is not meant to be purely theoretical but should be integrated into one's lived experience. By embodying and applying divine insights in daily life, individuals deepen their understanding and transform their consciousness.

In culmination, *theurgy* provides a scaffolding for the acquisition of *divine knowledge* through direct revelation, spiritual practices, symbolic language, and the harmonization of intellect and intuition. It recognizes that true knowledge extends beyond intellectual understanding and involves a transformation of consciousness and being. By aligning oneself with the divine, cultivating receptivity, and engaging in transformative practices, individuals can access revelatory insights and wisdom that originate from the *divine source* of knowledge. *Theurgy* highlights the ethical integration of *divine knowledge* and the transformative power of divine grace, inviting individuals to embody and manifest *divine wisdom* in their lives.

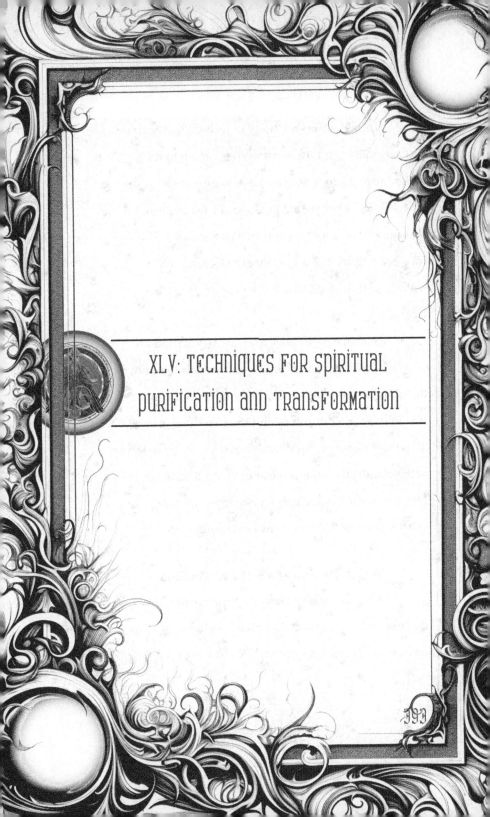

XLV: Techniques for Spiritual Purification and Transformation

Theurgy offers a variety of techniques for spiritual *purification* and transformation, aiming to refine the individual's consciousness and align it with the divine. While there may not be a specific Greek term for theurgical techniques for spiritual *purification* and transformation, we can explore the Greek term "κάθαρσις" (*katharsis*), which refers to *purification* or cleansing.

Spiritual *purification* and transformation are central to *theurgy*, as they enable individuals to remove the obstacles and impurities that hinder their connection with the divine and inhibit their spiritual growth. These techniques include various aspects of the individual, including the mind, emotions, body, and spirit. Here are some key techniques employed in *theurgy* for spiritual *purification* and transformation:

Self-Reflection and Self-Examination

Theurgy highlights the importance of self-reflection and self-examination as the initial steps in the process of spiritual *purification*. By observing and reflecting on one's thoughts, emotions, and behaviors, individuals can identify and understand the patterns, attachments, and bounds that prevent them from aligning with the divine.

Ethical Conduct

Theurgy recognizes the importance of ethical conduct in spiritual *purification*. Practicing virtues like honesty, compassion, integrity, and non-violence contributes to the *purification* of the individual's character and aligns their actions with higher principles. Ethical conduct nurtures harmony and integrity in one's relationships with others and with the divine.

Meditation and Mindfulness

Theurgy employs *meditation* and mindfulness practices to still the mind, encourage inner awareness, and detach from the fluctuations of thoughts and emotions. Through regular practice, individuals can develop clarity, focus, and a heightened sense of presence. *Meditation* also facilitates the recognition of the *divine presence* within and nurtures inner transformation.

Prayer and Devotion

Prayer and devotion are integral to *theurgy*'s spiritual *purification* techniques. Engaging in sincere and heartfelt prayer allows individuals to express their longing for *divine connection* and seek guidance and support in their spiritual quest. Devotion nurtures a deepening relationship with the divine and opens the heart to the transformative power of divine grace.

Rituals and Symbolic Acts

Rituals play a significant place in *theurgy*'s spiritual *purification* practices. Rituals involve symbolic acts that represent the individual's intention to purify and transform. Through rituals, individuals can symbolically release negative energies, patterns, and attachments while invoking divine blessings and guidance.

Breathwork and Pranayama

Theurgy incorporates breathwork and pranayama techniques to cleanse and purify the physical and energetic body. Conscious breathing exercises help to release stagnant energy, promote mental clarity, and restore balance to the body-mind system.

Pranayama practices facilitate the flow of life force energy (prana) and support the *purification* and expansion of consciousness.

Visualization and Imagery

Theurgy utilizes visualization and imagery techniques to transform and purify the individual's inner territory. By visualizing *divine light*, purifying energies, or transformative *symbols*, individuals can activate the power of the mind to effect positive change and release energetic blockages.

Sound and Mantra

The use of sound and mantra is another technique employed in *theurgy* for spiritual *purification* and transformation. Chanting sacred sounds, mantras, or divine names can help harmonize the energy centers, clear stagnant energy, and attune the individual to higher frequencies of consciousness. Sound vibrations have the power to purify and uplift the mind, emotions, and subtle energetic bodies.

Study of Sacred Texts

Theurgy recognizes the transformative power of studying sacred texts. Through the study and *contemplation* of spiritual scriptures, philosophical writings, and mystical teachings, individuals gain insights and wisdom that facilitate their spiritual *purification* and transformation. Sacred texts provide guidance, inspiration, and a deeper understanding of the divine principles.

Retreats and Solitude

Theurgy acknowledges the value of retreats and solitude in the process of spiritual *purification* and transformation. Temporarily withdrawing from external distractions and immersing oneself in a contemplative or solitary environment allows for introspection, reflection, and deepening of the spiritual connection. Retreats provide committed time and space for inner *work* and self-transformation.

Fasting and Dietary Practices

Theurgy recognizes the place of fasting and dietary practices in spiritual *purification*. Temporarily abstaining from certain foods or engaging in mindful eating practices can purify the body and mind, enhance clarity, and encourage a greater sensitivity to *divine energies*. Conscious dietary choices contribute to overall wellness and support the *purification* and transformation process.

Healing Modalities

Theurgy may incorporate various healing modalities, like energy healing, Reiki, acupuncture, or herbal medicine, to support the individual's spiritual *purification* and transformation. These modalities assist in clearing energetic imbalances, releasing emotional blockages, and facilitating the integration of physical, emotional, and spiritual aspects of the self.

Cultivation of Virtues

Theurgy highlights the cultivation of virtues as a means of spiritual *purification* and transformation. Virtues like humility, patience, forgiveness, gratitude, and love help to purify the heart and align the individual with *divine qualities*. The practice of virtues supports the embodiment of higher principles and nurtures spiritual growth and transformation.

Integration of Shadow Work

Theurgy acknowledges the importance of integrating the shadow aspects of the self for spiritual *purification* and transformation. Engaging in shadow *work* involves bringing to light and addressing repressed or unconscious aspects of one's personality. By embracing and integrating these aspects, individuals can experience greater wholeness, self-acceptance, and spiritual growth.

Spiritual Guidance and Mentorship

Theurgy recognizes the value of spiritual guidance and mentorship in the process of spiritual *purifica-*

tion and transformation. Seeking the support of a qualified spiritual teacher or mentor provides guidance, accountability, and a safe space for personal exploration and growth.

It is important to note that spiritual *purification* and transformation are ongoing processes that require commitment, intention, and perseverance. The combination of these techniques and practices in *theurgy* supports individuals in their quest toward greater alignment with the divine and the realization of their spiritual potential. By engaging in these practices, individuals can purify their consciousness, transform their lives, and deepen their connection with the divine.

XLVI: DIVINE LIGHT

The concept of *divine light* holds a significant place within *theurgy* and various mystical traditions. While there may not be a specific Greek term for the relationship between *theurgy* and the concept of *divine light*, we can explore the Greek term "φῶς" (phos), which signifies light in its literal and metaphorical sense.

In the context of *theurgy*, *divine light* refers to the radiant and luminous essence associated with the *divine presence*. It stands for the spiritual illumination, wisdom, and transformative power that emanates from the *divine world*. Here are some key insights into the place of *divine light* in *theurgy*:

Symbol of the Divine Presence

Divine light is often used as a *symbol* of the presence of the divine. It stands for the radiant energy and consciousness that permeates all of creation. *Theurgy* recognizes that the *divine light* is both immanent, existing within all things, and transcendent, emanating from a higher spiritual reality.

Illumination and Revelation

Divine light is associated with illumination and revelation. It is believed to unveil hidden truths, dispel ignorance, and bring forth spiritual insights. Through *theurgy*, individuals seek to attune themselves to the *divine light* in order to gain deeper understanding and wisdom.

Spiritual Transformation

Divine light is seen as a catalyst for spiritual transformation. It has the power to purify, heal, and uplift the individual's consciousness. By aligning with the *divine light*, individuals can undergo inner alchemy, experiencing a shift in their perception, values, and way of being.

Union with the Divine

Theurgy teaches that the experience of *divine light* is intertwined with the process of union with the divine. It is through merging with the *divine light* that individuals can attain a state of oneness and *transcen-*

dence. The experience of *divine light* is often described as a revelatory union with the *divine essence*.

Purification and Enlightenment

Divine light is associated with spiritual *purification* and enlightenment. It is believed to dissolve darkness, negativity, and impurities within the individual, illuminating the path toward spiritual growth and self-realization. The presence of *divine light* brings clarity, peace, and a sense of inner harmony.

Mystical Vision and Experience

Divine light is often encountered through mystical visions and experiences. It may manifest as a radiant glow, a brilliant aura, or an inner luminosity. *Theurgy* provides practices and techniques to encourage the capacity to perceive and commune with the *divine light*.

Healing and Wholeness

Divine light is believed to possess transformative and healing qualities. It can restore balance, harmony, and wholeness on physical, emotional, mental, and spiritual levels. *Theurgy* seeks to harness the power of *divine light* to facilitate healing and the integration of all aspects of the self.

Guidance and Protection

Divine light is seen as a source of guidance and protection. It illuminates the path and offers spiritual direction. *Theurgy* acknowledges the presence of *divine beings* and angelic forces associated with the *divine light*, offering their guidance and assistance on the spiritual quest.

Manifestation of Divine Qualities

Divine light is often associated with the manifestation of *divine qualities* like love, compassion, wisdom, and grace. It is through the infusion of *divine light* that individuals can embody and express these qualities in their lives. *Theurgy* provides practices that encourage the alignment with and emanation of *divine qualities*.

Inner Alchemy

Theurgy recognizes the transformative power of *divine light* in the process of inner alchemy. By consciously working with the *divine light*, individuals can transmute lower aspects of themselves into higher states of consciousness. The light acts as a catalyst for the refinement and elevation of the individual's spiritual essence.

Symbolic and Ritualistic Use

Theurgy employs various *symbols* and rituals to invoke, honor, and commune with the *divine light*. These practices can include visualizations, sacred gestures, incantations, and the use of sacred objects. *Theurgy* recognizes the power of intention and symbolic acts in attuning to the *divine light*.

Enmeshment and Unity

Divine light stands for the enmeshment and unity of all beings and the cosmos. It reminds individuals of their intrinsic connection to the divine and to each other. *Theurgy* seeks to encourage a consciousness that recognizes and honors this unity, leading to a sense of harmony and compassion.

In culmination, the concept of *divine light* holds a central place in *theurgy*, symbolizing the radiant essence of the divine, spiritual illumination, transformation, and union with the divine. It embodies qualities like wisdom, healing, guidance, and protection. Through practices and techniques, individuals can align themselves with the *divine light*, experiencing its transformative power, and integrating its qualities into their lives. The presence of *divine light* brings clarity, inspiration, and a deep sense of connection to the divine, encouraging spiritual growth, and the realization of one's true nature.

XLVII: DIVINE ORDER

The concept of *divine order* holds a significant place within *theurgy* and various mystical and philosophical traditions. While there may not be a specific Greek term for the relationship between *theurgy* and the concept of *divine order*, we can explore the Greek term "κόσμος" (kosmos), which signifies the harmonious arrangement, organization, and order of the universe.

In the context of *theurgy*, *divine order* refers to the inherent structure and organization that governs the cosmos and all its manifestations. It includes the underlying principles, patterns, and laws that bring about harmony, balance, and coherence in the world. Here are some key insights into the place of *divine order* in *theurgy*:

Harmony and Balance

Divine order is synonymous with harmony and balance. It reflects the perfect alignment and relationship of all elements, forces, and beings within the cosmos. *Theurgy* recognizes that when individuals align themselves with the principles of *divine order*, they experience a sense of harmony, coherence, and balance in their lives.

Alignment with Cosmic Rhythms

Divine order is associated with the rhythms and cycles that govern the universe. *Theurgy* teaches that by aligning oneself with these cosmic rhythms, individuals can attune to the natural flow of life and participate in the unfolding of *divine order*. This alignment brings a sense of purpose, meaning, and synchronicity.

Natural Laws and Principles

Divine order includes the natural laws and principles that govern the functioning of the universe. These laws include principles of cause and effect, interdependence, cycles of creation and dissolution, and the enmeshment of all. *Theurgy* highlights the understanding and alignment with these laws to facilitate personal and spiritual growth.

Manifestation of Divine Qualities

Divine order manifests through the expression of *divine qualities* like love, wisdom, compassion, and justice. It is through the alignment with these qualities that individuals can contribute to the establishment of *divine order* in their lives and in the world. *Theurgy* provides practices that encourage the embodiment and expression of these qualities.

Co-creation and Participation

Theurgy recognizes that individuals are co-creators within the *divine order*. Through conscious intention, aligned *action*, and harmonization with the divine, individuals participate in the unfolding of *divine order* and contribute to the manifestation of a more harmonious and balanced reality.

Ethical and Moral Alignment

Divine order includes ethical and moral principles that guide human behavior and interactions. *Theurgy* highlights the alignment with these principles as a means of harmonizing with the *divine order*. It recognizes that ethical conduct and moral choices are essential for creating and sustaining a harmonious and just world.

Cosmic Hierarchy and Divine Hierarchy

Divine order is often associated with *cosmic hierarchy* and the existence of a *divine hierarchy* of beings. *Theurgy* acknowledges the presence of various levels of existence and the enmeshment between these levels. It recognizes the place of *divine beings, angels,* and other spiritual forces in maintaining and sustaining the *divine order.*

Cultivation of Virtues

Theurgy recognizes the cultivation of virtues as a means of aligning with *divine order.* Virtues like wisdom, humility, patience, compassion, and integrity contribute to the establishment of harmonious relationships and the expression of *divine qualities.* The practice of virtues nurtures inner and outer alignment with the principles of *divine order.*

Rituals and Symbolic Acts

Rituals and symbolic acts play a significant place in *theurgy*'s engagement with *divine order*. Through rituals, individuals can honor, invoke, and align themselves with the principles of *divine order*. Symbolic acts, gestures, and sacred objects serve as reminders and conduits for the manifestation of *divine order* in daily life.

Acceptance of Divine Will

Theurgy highlights the acceptance of *divine will* as a fundamental aspect of aligning with *divine order*. It recognizes that surrendering to the greater intelligence and wisdom of the divine brings about a deeper sense of trust, peace, and alignment with the unfolding of *divine order*.

Spiritual Practices

Theurgy offers a range of spiritual practices to facilitate alignment with *divine order*. These practices include *meditation, contemplation,* prayer, *ritual, purification* techniques, and the cultivation of virtues. Through

these practices, individuals encourage the inner qualities and states of consciousness that are in harmony
with *divine order*.

Universal Love and Compassion

Divine order is sustained by universal love and
compassion. *Theurgy* highlights the cultivation of these
qualities as essential for aligning with *divine order* and
contributing to the wellness of all beings. Universal love
nurtures a sense of enmeshment, unity, and empathy,
which are necessary for the establishment of a harmonious and just world.

In culmination, the concept of *divine order* in
theurgy includes the inherent structure, organization,
and principles that govern the cosmos. It involves the
alignment with cosmic rhythms, natural laws, and ethical principles. Through practices of alignment, embodiment of *divine qualities*, and participation in co-creation,
individuals can contribute to the manifestation of *divine
order* in their lives and in the world. *Theurgy* recognizes
that alignment with *divine order* brings about harmony,

balance, and a deep sense of purpose and meaning. By attuning to the principles of *divine order*, individuals can experience a greater sense of enmeshment, inner peace, and alignment with the divine unfolding.

XLVIII: Neoplatonic Theories of the Afterlife

The place of *theurgy* in Neoplatonic theories of the afterlife is closely intertwined with the concept of *soul's quest* and the idea of ascent and union with the divine. While there may not be a specific Greek term for the relationship between *theurgy* and Neoplatonic theories of the afterlife, we can explore the Greek term "μετεμψύχωσις" (*metempsychosis*), which refers to the transmigration or reincarnation of the soul.

Neoplatonic theories of the afterlife, influenced by Plato's philosophy, posit that the soul is immortal and undergoes a quest beyond physical death. *Theurgy*, as a spiritual practice, holds an important place in preparing the soul for this quest and facilitating its ascent to higher realms of existence. Here are some key insights into the place of *theurgy* in Neoplatonic theories of the afterlife:

Soul's Quest and Divine Ascent

Neoplatonic theories posit that the *soul's quest* continues beyond physical death. *Theurgy* is seen as a means to prepare the soul for this quest and facilitate its ascent to higher realms of existence. The practices and techniques of *theurgy* aim to purify and refine the soul, enabling it to go beyond the bounds of the material world and reconnect with its divine origins.

Reunion with the Divine

The ultimate goal of *theurgy* in the context of the afterlife is the reunion of the soul with the divine. It is believed that the soul descends from the *divine world* into the material world and, through its quest and spiritual growth, seeks to reunite with its *divine source*. *Theurgy* provides a scaffolding and practices to facilitate this reunion and restore the soul's original state of union with the divine.

Purification and Spiritual Evolution

Theurgy recognizes the importance of spiritual *purification* and evolution in the *soul's quest* after death. It is believed that the soul carries with it the impressions, attachments, and experiences from its earthly existence. Through *theurgical practices*, the soul undergoes *purification*, shedding these bounds and attaining higher levels of consciousness and spiritual evolution.

Liberation from the Cycle of Birth and Death

Neoplatonic philosophy, including *theurgy*, seeks to liberate the soul from the cycle of birth and death, known as samsara. *Theurgy* sets its sights on helping the soul break free from the perpetual cycle of reincarnation and attain a state of spiritual liberation. By aligning with the divine and transcending the bounds of the material world, the soul can achieve liberation from the cycle of birth and death.

Preparing for the Afterlife

Theurgy provides practices and techniques to prepare the soul for the afterlife. These practices include *purification* rituals, *contemplation, meditation,* and the cultivation of virtues. By engaging in these practices, individuals can cleanse their consciousness, encourage spiritual qualities, and align themselves with the divine, thereby ensuring a more favorable quest beyond physical death.

Guidance and Protection

Theurgy acknowledges the presence of *divine beings*, angelic forces, and spiritual guides who assist the soul in its quest after death. Through *theurgical practices*, individuals seek the guidance and protection of these higher beings to navigate the realms of the afterlife and facilitate their ascent to higher states of existence.

Union with Higher Realms

Theurgy enables the soul to ascend to higher realms of existence. It is believed that the *soul's quest* after death involves encounters with various spiritual realms, each corresponding to different levels of consciousness and *divine presence*. The practices of *theurgy* facilitate the soul's ascent to these higher realms, leading to a deeper communion with the divine and a greater understanding of reality.

Integration of Divine Wisdom

Theurgy allows the soul to integrate *divine wisdom* acquired through its quest. As the soul ascends through the realms of existence, it gains deeper insights, understanding, and knowledge of the divine. *Theurgical practices* help the soul assimilate and integrate this wisdom, which contributes to its spiritual growth and evolution.

Liberation of the Divine Spark

Neoplatonic theories hold that each soul carries a divine spark within it. *Theurgy* wishes to facilitate the liberation and expansion of this divine spark, allowing it to merge with the *divine essence*. Through spiritual practices, the soul becomes a conduit for divine energy and realizes its inherent divinity.

Karmic Resolution

Theurgy recognizes the place of karma, the law of cause and effect, in the *soul's quest* after death. It is believed that the soul carries karmic imprints from past actions, which shape its experiences and determine its following incarnations. *Theurgical practices* assist in resolving karmic patterns, facilitating spiritual growth, and enabling the soul to go beyond the bounds imposed by past actions.

Integration of Personal and Universal Soul

Neoplatonic theories distinguish between the individual soul (personal soul) and the universal soul. *Theurgy* wishes to harmonize and integrate these aspects, enabling the individual soul to align with the universal soul and participate in the divine plan. By recognizing the enmeshment of all souls and the divine, *theurgy* nurtures a sense of unity and collective evolution.

In culmination, *theurgy* holds a necessary place in Neoplatonic theories of the afterlife by facilitating the *soul's quest*, *purification*, and ascent to higher realms of existence. The practices and techniques of *theurgy* prepare the soul for the afterlife, encourage spiritual qualities, and align the individual with the divine. Through *theurgy*, the soul seeks to reunite with the divine, go beyond the cycle of birth and death, and attain

liberation and union with the higher realms of existence.

XLIX: THEORIES OF THE AFTERLIFE COMPARED TO OTHER ESOTERICA

The concept of the afterlife has been a fundamental aspect of various esoteric religious systems and philosophical traditions throughout history. Among these, Neoplatonism stands out as a unique and influential system of thought, offering revelatory insights into the nature of the *soul's quest* beyond physical death. This essay searches out Neoplatonic theories of the afterlife and compares them to other esoteric religious systems' perspectives on the subject.

Neoplatonic Theories of the Afterlife

Neoplatonism, founded by the philosopher Plotinus in the 3rd century CE, draws heavily from the teachings of Plato. It posits that the soul descends from *the One*, the ineffable source of all existence, into the material world, and its ultimate goal is to reunite with the divine. The *soul's quest* is marked by a process of *purification* and ascent, guided by *theurgy* and spiritual practices.

According to Neoplatonic theories, the soul is immortal and undergoes a cycle of reincarnation known as *metempsychosis*. The experiences of each lifetime shape the soul's evolution and understanding, leading it closer to the *divine essence*. *Theurgy* holds a significant place in the *soul's quest* by purifying its essence, aligning it with higher spiritual forces, and facilitating its ascent to higher realms of existence.

Neoplatonic thought highlights the place of knowledge and intellectual understanding in the *soul's quest*. The soul gains insights into higher realities through *contemplation* and direct experiential knowledge, transcending the bounds of the material world.

Egyptian Mysticism and the Afterlife

In ancient Egyptian religion and mysticism, the afterlife held immense importance. The Egyptians believed in the concept of an eternal soul known as the "ka," which continued to exist after death. To ensure a favorable afterlife, the deceased underwent a process of mummification and burial rituals.

The Book of the Dead, a collection of funerary texts, acted as a guide for the *soul's quest* through the afterlife. The deceased's heart was weighed against the feather of Ma'at, symbolizing truth and justice. If the heart was found pure and free of wrongdoing, the soul would proceed to the afterlife and attain eternal life.

Hindu Beliefs on Reincarnation and Liberation

Hinduism, one of the oldest and most diverse religious systems, revolves around the concepts of karma, dharma, and reincarnation. According to Hindu beliefs, the soul, known as the "atman," undergoes a cycle of birth and rebirth, influenced by the law of karma. The quality of one's actions and intentions in previous lives determines the circumstances of their next reincarnation.

Hinduism posits that the ultimate goal of life is to break free from the cycle of reincarnation, attain liberation or "moksha," and reunite with the cosmic consciousness, Brahman. Various spiritual practices, including *meditation*, yoga, and devotion, are prescribed to purify the soul and achieve spiritual realization.

Tibetan Buddhism and the Bardo Thodol

In Tibetan Buddhism, the afterlife is explored through the teachings of the Bardo Thodol, commonly known as the Tibetan Book of the Dead. The Bardo Thodol acts as a guide for the *soul's quest* through the intermediate state between death and rebirth, known as the bardo.

During the bardo, the soul experiences various visionary states, encountering peaceful and wrathful *deities*. The purpose of the Bardo Thodol is to provide instructions for the deceased to navigate these states and attain liberation from the cycle of reincarnation.

Hermeticism and the Quest for Immortality

Hermeticism, an esoteric philosophical tradition influenced by ancient Egyptian and Greek thought, places great emphasis on the quest for spiritual immortality. The Hermetic texts, attributed to the mythical figure Hermes Trismegistus, offer insights into the nature of the soul and its ascent to higher realms.

Hermeticism shares similarities with Neoplatonism in its belief in the *divine origin* of the soul and its potential for spiritual elevation. The practice of alchemy, a central aspect of Hermeticism, wishes to transform the soul and attain spiritual perfection.

Islamic Mysticism and the Quest of the Soul

Islamic mysticism, known as Sufism, dives into the quest of the soul towards *divine union*. Sufis believe in the immortality of the soul and its return to the *divine source* after death.

Sufi practices, like Sufi whirling and devotional *poetry*, aim to facilitate the soul's ascent and *purification*. Sufism places great importance on the individual's direct experience of the *divine presence*, leading to a revelatory spiritual transformation.

Gnostic Views on Salvation and the Afterlife

Gnosticism, an ancient religious and philosophical movement, offers unique perspectives on salvation and the afterlife. Gnostic texts portray the material world as a world of illusion and suffering, with the soul trapped in the physical body.

Salvation, in Gnostic thought, involves the awakening of the divine spark within the soul, enabling it to go beyond the material world and reunite with the divine. Gnostic practices emphasize the acquisition of esoteric knowledge as a means to attain liberation from the constraints of the material world.

Comparative Analysis

Neoplatonic theories of the afterlife share commonalities with other esoteric religious systems regarding the soul's immortality, the importance of spiritual *purification*, and the quest for *divine union*. The concept of reincarnation or *metempsychosis* is prevalent in many of these traditions, emphasizing the *soul's quest* through different lifetimes.

Theurgy, as a central aspect of Neoplatonism, bears some resemblance to the practices of other esoteric systems, like Egyptian mysticism's rituals and Tibetan Buddhism's Bardo Thodol. These practices serve to guide the soul through the afterlife, facilitate spiritual growth, and ultimately lead to liberation.

However, some distinctions emerge in the way these systems approach the afterlife and the *soul's quest*. Neoplatonism stands out with its emphasis on intellectual understanding and direct experiential knowledge as paths to divine realization. While other traditions may value knowledge and mystical insights, they may also rely on rituals, devotion, or specific practices for spiritual growth.

Hinduism's belief in the law of karma and the concept of moksha aligns with the idea of spiritual *purification* and liberation found in Neoplatonic theories. However, Hinduism places greater emphasis on fulfilling one's dharma or duty in life as a means to accumulate positive karma and attain spiritual growth.

In contrast, Hermeticism and Gnosticism share a focus on the transformation of the soul and its potential for spiritual elevation. These traditions emphasize the quest for spiritual immortality and *divine knowledge*, with Gnosticism particularly highlighting the soul's awakening to its true divine nature.

Tibetan Buddhism's Bardo Thodol and Islamic Sufism's practices offer unique approaches to the afterlife and the *soul's quest*. Tibetan Buddhism provides detailed guidance for navigating the intermediate state between death and rebirth, while Sufism centers on the individual's direct experience of *divine presence* as a means to attain spiritual transformation.

In culmination, Neoplatonic theories of the afterlife present a compelling and distinctive perspective on the *soul's quest* beyond physical death. The concept of *theurgy*, spiritual *purification*, and intellectual understanding as paths to *divine union* sets Neoplatonism apart from other esoteric religious systems.

L: COMPARING AND CONTRASTING WITH OTHER ESOTERIC TRADITIONS

Theurgy and Neoplatonic Mysticism, along with various esoteric religious systems, have contributed to the valuable atlas of human spirituality and understanding of the afterlife and the *soul's quest*. Each of these traditions brings forth unique perspectives on spiritual growth, *purification*, and *divine union*. In this comparison, we will explore some key aspects of these diverse traditions and how they intersect with the concepts of *theurgy* and Neoplatonic mysticism.

Hermeticism and Alchemy in Renaissance Europe

Hermeticism, influenced by ancient Egyptian and Greek thought, emerged during the Renaissance in Europe. It highlights the quest for spiritual immortality and the transformation of the soul. Similar to Neoplatonism, Hermeticism highlights the *divine origin* of the soul and its potential for elevation through spiritual practices and alchemical transmutation.

Alchemy, a central aspect of Hermeticism, involves the symbolic *purification* and transformation of base metals into gold, mirroring the *soul's quest* towards spiritual perfection. Both *theurgy* and alchemy seek to unlock hidden truths and attain spiritual insights, ultimately leading to *divine union* and enlightenment.

Gnosticism: Ancient Mystical Traditions, Sects & Texts

Gnosticism presents a diverse array of mystical traditions and texts that dive into the nature of the soul and its relationship with the divine. Like Neoplatonism, Gnosticism places great importance on direct experiential knowledge and insight into higher realities. Both traditions emphasize the place of the soul's enlightenment and liberation from the constraints of the material world.

However, Gnosticism differs from *theurgy* in its dualistic worldview, considering the material world as a world of illusion and suffering, while the spiritual world is the domain of the divine. *Theurgy*, on the other hand, seeks to purify the soul and elevate it, considering the material world as a stepping stone towards divine realization.

Zoroastrianism: Esoteric Teachings and the Priesthood of the Fire

Zoroastrianism, an ancient Persian religion, highlights the dualistic struggle between good and evil. The *soul's quest* in Zoroastrianism is guided by the concept of divine judgment, where the righteous attain a blissful afterlife, and the wicked face punishment. This idea shares similarities with the Neoplatonic emphasis on the soul's *purification* and ascent towards *divine union*.

The priesthood of the fire holds a necessary place in Zoroastrianism, conducting sacred rituals and maintaining the sacred fire. These practices align with theurgical techniques in Neoplatonism, where rituals and invocations are employed to invoke *divine energies* and purify the soul.

Sufism: Persian Mystical Path of Islam

Sufism, the mystical path of Islam, focuses on attaining direct experiences of the divine through practices like *meditation*, chanting, and ecstatic dancing. Similar to theurgical techniques, Sufi practices seek to go beyond the ego and unite with the divine.

Both Neoplatonism and Sufism highlight the importance of *divine love* and the soul's longing for union with the divine. However, Sufism, being within the context of Islam, incorporates Islamic theology and the teachings of the Quran into its mystical practices.

Daoist Immortality and Internal Alchemy

Daoist teachings in ancient China revolve around the quest for immortality and spiritual transformation. Daoist practitioners seek to harmonize with the Tao, the fundamental principle that underlies all existence. Internal alchemy, a core Daoist practice, involves refining and purifying the internal energies to achieve longevity and spiritual enlightenment.

In comparison, *theurgy* and Neoplatonic mysticism also advocate spiritual *purification* and ascent towards the divine. Both traditions emphasize the soul's potential for spiritual growth and seek to go beyond the bounds of the material world.

Shamanism in Siberia: Animism and Nature Worship

Siberian shamanism includes a range of animistic beliefs and practices involving communication with spirits and nature worship. Shamans act as intermediaries between the human world and the spirit world, performing rituals and invocations to maintain harmony and balance.

While *theurgy* and Neoplatonic mysticism differ in their emphasis on intellectual understanding and direct experiential knowledge, both traditions share a reverence for the spiritual world and realize the enmeshment of all.

African Traditional Religions and Spirituality

African traditional religions include a huge array of beliefs and practices, emphasizing ancestor worship, reverence for nature, and communication with spirits. *Theurgy* and Neoplatonic mysticism offer contrasting approaches, with *theurgy* sharpening on spiritual *purification* and intellectual understanding, while

African traditional religions emphasizing *ritual* practices and communal spirituality.

Despite their differences, both traditions acknowledge the revelatory enmeshment between the human and spiritual realms, affirming the importance of the *soul's quest* towards the divine.

Druidism and Celtic Mysticism

Druidism, the ancient spiritual tradition of the Celtic peoples, centers on nature worship, the reverence of ancestors, and the pursuit of wisdom. Celtic mysticism shares similarities with *theurgy* and Neoplatonic mysticism, as both traditions realize the transformative power of spiritual practices and the pursuit of higher truths.

Druids and theurgists alike seek to unlock hidden knowledge and insights through their rituals and practices, guiding the soul towards divine understanding and enlightenment.

Indigenous Australian Dreamtime, Songlines, and Ancestral Beings

Indigenous Australian spirituality revolves around the Dreamtime, a mythical era when ancestral beings shaped the land and established cultural norms. Songlines, complex narratives that traverse the territory, connect the people to their ancestral heritage and the spiritual dimensions of the land.

Theurgy and Neoplatonic mysticism emphasize the importance of direct experiential knowledge and the pursuit of divine truths. However, the Indigenous Australian spirituality focuses on the oral transmission of ancestral stories and cultural practices to connect with the spiritual realms.

Jyotish: Vedic Astrology

Jyotish, or Vedic *astrology*, is an ancient Indian system of *astrology* that seeks to understand and influence the cosmic energies to enhance one's life. It highlights the relationship between the planetary positions and human destinies.

Theurgy and Neoplatonic mysticism, on the other hand, emphasize the *purification* of the soul and its ascent to higher realms, with *theurgy* employing rituals and invocations to invoke *divine energies*.

Theurgy and Neoplatonic mysticism stand as unique and revelatory spiritual paths, emphasizing the *soul's quest* towards *divine union* through spiritual *purification* and intellectual understanding. By comparing and contrasting these traditions with various esoteric religious systems worldwide, we can appreciate the richness and diversity of human spirituality and its pursuit of higher truths and enlightenment. Each tradition brings forth a unique approach to the afterlife, the *soul's quest*, and the quest for *divine wisdom*, contributing to humanity's spiritual evolution and understanding of the cosmos.

CULMINATION

In culmination, the exploration of *theurgy* and Neoplatonic mysticism alongside a wide array of esoteric religious systems has unveiled a fascinating atlas of human spirituality. Each tradition brings forth unique insights into the *soul's quest*, the afterlife, and the quest for higher truths and enlightenment. The common threads that combine these diverse traditions together are the pursuit of *divine union*, spiritual *purification*, and the understanding of the interconnection between the material and spiritual realms.

Throughout history and across cultures, humanity has tried to comprehend the mysteries of existence, the nature of the soul, and its relationship with the divine. From ancient Egypt to modern-day Vodou in Haiti, from Neoplatonic philosophers to Sufi mystics, seekers of *divine wisdom* and spiritual illumination have utilized various rituals, practices, and *symbols* to bridge the gap between the material and spiritual dimensions.

The concept of *theurgy*, with its emphasis on invoking divine powers and purifying the soul through sacred rituals, is a recurring theme in many mystical traditions. Theurgical techniques have been employed in different ways to connect with higher realities, gain spiritual insights, and attain unity with the divine. Whether through Hermeticism's alchemical transmutation, Sufism's ecstatic dancing, or Daoism's internal alchemy, practitioners have tried to achieve spiritual transformation and divine illumination.

Moreover, the Neoplatonic philosophy of Plotinus significantly influenced the development of *theurgy*. Plotinus's emphasis on the soul's *divine origin* and its ascent towards *the One* aligns with *theurgical practices*, emphasizing the *purification* of the soul and its reunion with the *divine source*. The Neoplatonic view of the universe as a hierarchical structure, with different levels of reality, further reinforces the importance of the *soul's quest* through these realms.

Throughout this exploration, we have encountered numerous mystical traditions, each offering its unique understanding of the afterlife. From the Zoroastrian emphasis on divine judgment to the Gnostic perception of the material world as an illusion, these beliefs shape how individuals approach death and the concept of the afterlife. Neoplatonic theories of the afterlife, with their focus on the soul's *purification* and ascent, vibe with many of these traditions, as seekers aim to go beyond the bounds of the material world and unite with the divine.

Furthermore, the emphasis on *divine love*, grace, and wisdom in *theurgical practices* aligns with the universal themes of many mystical traditions. Whether in Sufism's devotion to the Beloved, Kabbalah's pursuit of *divine wisdom*, or Christian *theurgy's invocation* of divine grace, these traditions realize the transformative power of *divine qualities* in the *soul's quest* towards unity.

The concept of spiritual protection and defense, seen in theurgical techniques, also finds parallels in various traditions' practices, like Shamanism's communication with spirits for guidance and protection or African traditional religions' use of rituals to ward off malevolent forces. These practices reflect the universal human desire for safety and spiritual guidance in the face of unseen forces.

Moreover, the relationship between *theurgy* and magic reveals complex connections between mystical practices and the manipulation of natural forces. While some traditions distinguish between *theurgy* as a divine and beneficial practice and magic as a potentially harmful manipulation of power, the lines can often be blurry. Both *theurgy* and magic reflect human attempts to interact with higher realities and influence the natural world through rituals and *symbols*.

The integration of *theurgy* and philosophy in Neoplatonism has had a revelatory effect on the development of Western esoteric traditions. The emphasis on intellectual understanding and direct experiential knowledge vibes with many mystical paths, as seekers strive to attain wisdom and insight into reality and the divine.

Furthermore, *theurgical practices* have breathed *art*, *architecture*, literature, and *music* in various cultures throughout history. These creative expressions serve as vehicles for conveying mystical experiences, divine insights, and spiritual truths. From the symbolism of

Egyptian temples to the *poetry* of Sufi mystics, *theurgy-*breathed *art* and literature endure to allure and inspirit seekers of *divine wisdom*.

The concept of *divine names and attributes* is another essential aspect shared by many mystical traditions. The use of sacred names and invocations to access divine energies is prevalent in *theurgical practices*, as seen in the Jewish Kabbalah's exploration of the divine names or Hindu Tantra's use of bija mantras. The understanding that divine names carry potent spiritual power is a common thread that weaves through mystical paths worldwide.

Theurgy's relationship with *astrology* and its use of *talismans* and *amulets* to harness cosmic energies reflect the enmeshment of the microcosm and macrocosm. From Vedic *astrology* to Hellenistic astrological practices, these traditions realize the influence of celestial bodies on human destinies and seek to align with cosmic rhythms.

In the quest for spiritual illumination and enlightenment, theurgical techniques, like *meditation*, visualization, and ecstatic practices, find resonance in numerous mystical paths. From the transcendental meditations of Hindu yogis to the ecstatic dances of Sufi dervishes, seekers have employed various methods to achieve altered states of consciousness and unite with the divine.

The concept of *divine truth*, an essential theme in *theurgical practices*, is central to the pursuit of higher wisdom in many mystical traditions. Whether seeking gnosis in Gnosticism, understanding the divine mysteries in Kabbalah, or recognizing the enmeshment of all in Indigenous Australian Dreamtime, the quest for *divine truth* is a driving force in the *soul's quest* towards enlightenment.

Divine harmony, another recurrent theme in *theurgical practices*, is also evident in the emphasis on balance and unity in many mystical traditions. From the Daoist pursuit of harmonizing with the Tao to the Indigenous African belief in the enmeshment of all living beings, seekers of *divine wisdom* realize the importance of living in harmony with the natural order.

Throughout this exploration, we have encountered numerous esoteric religious systems, each offering its unique perspective on the *soul's quest* and the pursuit of higher truths and spiritual enlightenment. From the mysteries of Ancient Egyptian rituals to the revelations of the Kabbalistic Tree of Life, these diverse traditions represent humanity's revelatory and lasting quest for *divine wisdom* and union.

In culmination, *theurgy* and Neoplatonic mysticism stand as revelatory and significant spiritual paths in the broader context of esoteric religious systems. The convergence of these traditions with various mystical paths worldwide reveals the enmeshment of human spirituality and the universal quest for higher truths and enlightenment. While each tradition brings forth unique practices and perspectives, the common themes of spiritual *purification, divine union*, and the pursuit of wisdom bind them together in the eternal quest of the soul towards the divine. As humanity keeps exploring the mysteries of existence, *theurgy* and Neoplatonic mysticism will undoubtedly endure as lasting sources of inspiration and guidance in the eternal quest for *divine truth* and illumination.

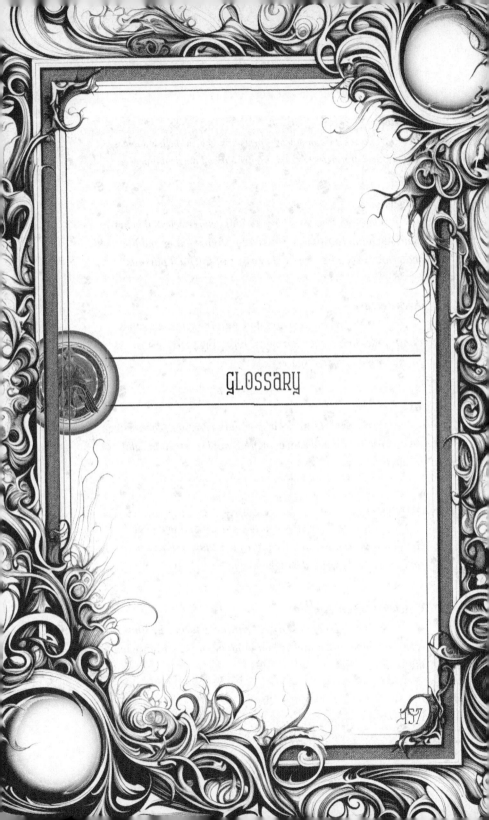

GLOSSARY

Amulets

"αμουλέτα" (amouléta) - protective charms believed to possess mystical properties that aid in spiritual and magical practices

Angels

are referred to as "άγγελοι" (ángeloi) - celestial beings considered intermediaries between the divine realm and the material world, often invoked to assist in spiritual pursuits

Architecture

is "αρχιτεκτονική" (architektoniki) - symbolizes the divine order and cosmic harmony, reflecting sacred principles in the design of sacred spaces

Art

is "τέχνη" (téchnē) - a spiritual expression, channeling divine inspiration and conveying profound mystical insights through creative endeavors

Asceticism

"ασχηση" (askísi) - rigorous self-discipline and abstention from worldly indulgences as a means to purify the soul and attain spiritual enlightenment

Celestial intelligences

divine beings or spiritual entities associated with the celestial realms, often invoked for guidance and assistance in mystical practices

Contemplation

a deep and focused meditative state where the practitioner seeks to connect with divine realities and higher truths

Cosmic Hierarchy / Great Chain of Being

a hierarchical order of existence, ranging from the highest divine entities down to the material world, reflecting the interconnectedness and gradation of cosmic levels

Deities

Deity is "θεότητα" (theótita) - divine beings or gods worshipped and revered for their spiritual significance and connection to the transcendent realm

Divination

"μαντεία" (manteía) - the practice of seeking insights into future events or hidden knowledge through spiritual or mystical means

Divine beauty

the perception of spiritual harmony and perfection, reflecting the radiant qualities of the divine realm

Divine communion

the mystical union or direct connection with the divine, often achieved through spiritual practices and rituals.

Divine connection

the mystical and spiritual bond established between the practitioner and the divine, fostering a direct communion with higher realms and divine energies

Divine drama

the sacred rituals and symbolic enactments that mirror cosmic principles and allow participants to commune with divine forces and archetypal energies

Divine energies

spiritual forces or emanations believed to flow from the divine realm and are harnessed in mystical practices to achieve spiritual transformation and communion with the divine

Divine emanation

the process through which divine energy, wisdom, or spiritual essence flows and manifests from the higher realms into the material world

Divine essence

the fundamental nature and core attributes of the divine, believed to be accessible through spiritual practices for transformative experiences

Divine forces

the transcendent powers and energies that are believed to influence and shape spiritual experiences and transformations

Divine harmony

the state of perfect alignment and balance within the spiritual realm, reflecting the interconnectedness and unity of all divine elements

Divine inspiration

the influx of spiritual guidance or creative ideas believed to be bestowed upon an individual by higher spiritual beings or the divine realm

Divine intelligence

the transcendent wisdom and knowledge attributed to celestial beings or spiritual forces, which seekers may invoke to gain insights and spiritual understanding

Divine knowledge

spiritual insights and wisdom attained through direct communion with the divine, often sought after in mystical practices

Divine light

a spiritual illumination or inner radiance that represents the presence and guidance of higher spiritual forces

Divine names and attributes

sacred appellations and qualities ascribed to the divine, often invoked for spiritual communion and transformative experiences

Divine order

the harmonious and structured arrangement of the cosmos, reflecting the inherent organization and purposefulness in the divine plan

Divine origin

the belief that certain spiritual principles, beings, or experiences have their source in the divine realm or are derived from the divine essence

Divine presence

the palpable and direct experience of the divine essence or spiritual energy during mystical practices or sacred rituals

Divine providence

the belief in the benevolent guidance and care of the divine over the course of human affairs and spiritual development

Divine purposes

the higher intentions or plans of the divine realm, which practitioners seek to align with through spiritual practices

Divine qualities

the transcendental attributes or virtues associated with the divine, sought to be embodied or realized by the practitioner in their spiritual journey

Divine realms

spiritual planes or dimensions believed to be inhabited by celestial beings and divine intelligences, accessible through mystical practices

Divine source

the ultimate origin and wellspring of all spiritual power and wisdom, serving as the foundation for mystical practices and communion with the divine

Divine truth

the ultimate and transcendent knowledge that reveals the fundamental nature of reality and the divine essence

Divine union

the ultimate spiritual goal, where the practitioner seeks to merge their consciousness with the divine or higher realms, achieving a profound and transformative connection with the divine source

Divine will

the higher purpose or intention of the divine, which practitioners seek to align with and fulfill through spiritual practices

Divine wisdom

profound spiritual insights and knowledge believed to originate from the divine source, guiding seekers towards enlightenment and understanding

Eucharist

also known as Holy Communion, *is a sacred ritual or sacrament in Christian traditions where participants partake in bread and wine, symbolizing the spiritual presence and unity with the divine*

Icons

sacred images or representations of divine beings, serving as objects of veneration and focal points for spiritual devotion and connection

Invocations

"επίχλησι" (epíklisi) - ritualistic prayers or calls to divine beings, seeking their presence and assistance in spiritual practices.

Jesus Prayer

a repetitive prayer that invokes the name of Jesus as a means of achieving spiritual concentration and communion with the divine

Meditation

a practice of quieting the mind and entering a state of profound inner stillness, allowing for communion with divine energies and spiritual insights

Metanoia

   a transformative change of heart and mind, leading to spiritual growth and a closer alignment with divine principles

Music

   "μουσική" (mousikē) - a powerful tool for invoking spiritual energies and facilitating transcendent experiences during mystical practices.

Oracles

   individuals, places, or methods through which divine messages or insights are believed to be conveyed, often consulted for spiritual guidance and prophetic revelations

Pentagram

   a five-pointed star symbol representing the five elements (earth, water, air, fire, and spirit) and is often used for protective and spiritual purposes

Poetry is "ποίηση" (poíēsē)

   a sacred and inspired form of expression, channeling spiritual insights and divine revelations through rhythmic and symbolic language

Prophecy

   "προφητεία" (propheteía) - the mystical practice of receiving divine revelations or insights about future events or spiritual truths.

Purification

"κάθαρσις" (kátharsis) - the process of cleansing and purifying the soul from impurities, allowing for a closer connection with the divine and spiritual transformation

Quest

"ταξίδι" (taxídi) - a spiritual journey or pilgrimage undertaken by the practitioner to seek divine knowledge, wisdom, or enlightenment

Ritual

"τελετή" (teletí) - sacred ceremonies and prescribed practices that facilitate spiritual communion with the divine and the realization of mystical goals

Sacred hymns

devotional songs or chants imbued with spiritual significance, often used to invoke and honor divine forces during mystical practices

Symbol is "σύμβολον" (sýmbolon)

a sacred representation or sign used to convey hidden spiritual meanings and facilitate communication with the divine realm

Talismans "ταλισμάνι" (talismaní)

consecrated objects believed to possess spiritual powers and protect the wearer from negative influences or attract divine blessings

Theia Hierarchia

"Θεία Ιεραρχία" - the divine hierarchy or sacred order of celestial beings, each possessing specific roles and responsibilities in the spiritual realm.

Theurgy

theourgia (Θεουργία) - spiritual practices and rituals aimed at invoking and uniting with divine powers to achieve mystical transformation and union with the divine.

To Hen Το Εν

the philosophical concept of "The One" or the ultimate, transcendent, and indivisible source of all existence

Transcendence

the spiritual state of rising above ordinary existence, reaching a higher level of consciousness, and connecting with divine or cosmic realms

Transit astrology

the study of planetary movements and their influence on an individual's life and spiritual journey.

World Soul

Anima Mundi - the divine and universal soul believed to animate and interconnect all living beings and the entire cosmos.

Ω

OMEGA

Dear student of the **Esoteric Religious Studies Series**, we express our deepest gratitude for departing on this enlightening adventure. Having dived into the realms of esoteric *wisdom*, may you carry the flame of knowledge within your being. May the insights gained and the revelations experienced guide your path as you traverse the atlas of life. May the *wisdom* you have acquired permeate every aspect of your existence, nurturing your spirit and triggering your actions. May you carry on to seek truth, look favorably towards growth, and walk the path of *wisdom* with grace and compassion. May your life be a confirmation of the transformative power of esoteric knowledge.

If you have enjoyed the words of this book, please consider leaving a review in the marketplace you found it so that its content can enrich the lives of others.

OTHER BOOKS IN THIS SERIES

A WORLD OF ESOTERIC THOUGHT

ISBN: 979-8-85-338673-0